Lost Edens

Lost Edens

A True Story

JAMIE PATTERSON

ISBN: 978-1-59298-386-5
Library of Congress Control Number: 2011921713

Printed in the United States of America
First Printing: 2012

16   15   14   13   12   5   4   3   2   1

Book design by Ryan Scheife, Mayfly Design

BEAVER'S POND
PRESS

Beaver's Pond Press, Inc.
7104 Ohms Lane, Suite 101, Edina, MN 55439-2129
(952) 829-8818 · www.BeaversPondPress.com
To order, visit www.BeaversPondBooks.com
or call (800) 901-3480. Reseller discounts available.

Ted comes to visit and I can't help longing for lost Edens.

—SYLVIA PLATH

1

WINDING ROAD

My grandfather remembers this stretch of road as two thin strips of gravel. A line of grass growing down the middle, lending a straight line all the way from the main dirt road to the lake. His father, my great-grandfather, made the road himself. Plucking the trees one by one, he had cleared a winding path that eased past blueberry fields and sparkling blue water on either side.

The lake was, all but a small corner, his.

I'm here now, just back from California, at the lake in the woods my great-grandfather helped form. I like to imagine him looking into a deep forest and planning this road. Now it is all gravel, the grass relegated to the sides. The blueberry fields are gone, and here and there cabins block the view to the lake.

The road is mine for the taking, and I'm glad for the solitude. The gravel road is bumpy beneath my sandaled feet, making me wish for the tennis shoes that are somewhere between San Diego and Minneapolis packed away in a moving truck.

Kicking rocks down the road, I don't care that my feet will be dusty and brown from the exposure. My dog, Huey, is in the woods, having found something spectacular to dig his nose in, and I don't care much that he'll bring the special stench of that spot home with him.

A car is crackling over the gravel down the road in front of me, sending billows of brown dust into the summer air. I turn my head to the thick sun-kissed trees so the car passengers won't see my tears as they pass.

I can see through the woods to the cabin my great-grandfather built with his own hands. Standing steady after all these years, it sat on this peninsula, in these woods, long before me.

Huey gives up on his special spot and is running toward the cabin, leaping through the woods. I have to smile at his enthusiasm for the new scenery. If only for his sake and safety I know I should be glad for the circumstance.

The sun is beating down hard on my tanned arms, and as it sears the top of my head I silently hope that it will work to keep my hair as blond as the California sun did. It's good, I think to myself, to have such shallow thoughts right now. It's a good thing.

I'm still thinking this as I step into the shade to follow Huey closer to my great-grandfather's cabin. Before reaching the main cabin, I have to pass Harry's place. A small, one-bedroom structure perched precariously on a small hill overlooking the lake. Harry was the caretaker for my great-grandfather. Year-round on this lake in the middle of Minnesota, he maintained the main cabin, and ensured the road was passable. For years, through snow and rain, Harry was often the only living human for miles.

I wish Harry were here, I think, looking at the carefully laid stone pathway leading from his door to the clearing in front of the main cabin. I don't know much about his life but know enough to say with certainty he wasn't a stranger to pain. Sitting isolated in the middle of a white Minnesota winter, he had slowly gone mad before taking his own life.

"You would know how to talk to me," I say to his small, tilting home.

Looking back to the main road I know I should start the walk back to my parents' cabin. It's the middle of July, but I'm not sure of what time it is, or when the sun sets in Minnesota.

Huey isn't done exploring, and I'm not done crying, so I keep walking toward my great-grandfather's cabin, and to the very tip of the peninsula.

There are Indian burial mounds here at the outermost point of the peninsula. I wonder if I ask them to, if the spirits of those beneath the earth will talk to me. I'm in so much pain, this doesn't seem like an unreasonable idea.

"Hello?" I call. "Can you hear me?"

Nothing but the breaking of leaves under Huey's feet.

"I could really, really use some help," I say through tears, looking to my left and right for a sign of response.

For a moment, I know how I must appear to any living creature that might hear me, and I look for evidence of life.

Huey is poised, watching loons bob in the water just off the nearby beach. I'm surrounded by woods, which are surrounded by water, and I know the closest person wouldn't hear me if I screamed. And I want to. I want to scream at the woods, and scream at God, and scream at the Indian spirits for not talking back to me. I want to scream at Ben, my husband. I want to scream at my younger self to choose differently.

I don't scream, though.

Instead, I cry. I drop to my knees, put my head in

my hands, and cry. Huey isn't sure if I'm beckoning him, and he comes to sniff at my hair, which covers my hands and my face. We sit here like this, Huey and I, waiting for reason to move. Huey's comes first, in the form of a chipmunk. Mine comes next with the need for open space. My pain is too big for these enclosed woods. I need room, I need the ocean I left behind, I need endless sky above. I need an enduring semblance of eternity.

My great-grandfather's road will do.

Running through the woods, the wide-open space around the main cabin is a relief, but I don't stop. Past Harry's, cutting through a thick of birch trees, I burst onto the gravel and stop.

My breathing is hard, my vision is blurry, my chest squeezed as though something has twisted its way around it.

"What do you want from me?" I say to my great-grandfather's road. I don't care who hears.

"Here I am! You got me here, now what do you want?"

No reply.

"Huh? What do you want?" I scream this time. Huey stops his investigation along the side of the road and looks to me, waiting.

The tears won't stop. My hand shakes hard as I wipe my face and nose. I don't mind the sobbing right now. I know that as soon as I'm in my parents' cabin I'll have to make some effort to control my desperation. My family, I know, is weary of my struggle. It's been their struggle, too.

"Good boy, come on," I say to Huey. The summer sky is slowly turning gray, and it won't be long before the road is enveloped with thick darkness. Instead of coming, Huey slowly lowers his hind legs to sit and watches me.

"Let's go," I say, annoyed. The tears haven't stopped.

Turning toward my parents' cabin, the idea of my grandfather walking down the middle grassy stretch of this road is no longer comforting like it used to be. The idea that some of these trees were the same trees that looked down on my father as a young boy, or me as a little girl, is no longer comforting like it used to be.

The vast continuum of time has stopped. The natural progression of my life has stopped. It matters not to me right now that this road, and these trees, will outlive my pain, outlive me.

2

BEACH COTTAGE

Three weeks earlier, California

It's the Fourth of July. I get to move into my beach cottage as soon as I get up, so I wake in the early morning hours to pack. I don't have much to move from my brother's house in Ocean Beach, up the Pacific coastline to my new home. Which is good. My 1969 red Fiat Roadster convertible can't hold much more than what clothes I have left, and my brother promises to help with the rest once he checks the surf.

I'm anxious to get moving, and I don't really want my brother to know where I'll be living. Either Ben can know where I live and no one else, or my family can know and Ben can't. I am choosing Ben. I am choosing my husband.

The crowds will be thick today along La Jolla Shores, my new home, for the holiday. Watching my brother's back as he walks the long block from his house to the beach I stand impatient, waiting, ready to move on. I think for a moment about leaving. Jumping in the shining red Fiat to head north on my own. My brother doesn't know where the cottage is, and I know I can get away with disappearing for a few hours. My brother has been so good, though, and I need the help. I need to be moved in and ready if Ben calls.

I check to make sure pillows and sweaters are neatly tucked in so the winds won't send them flying across Highway 5. I check to make sure my gearshift can be used beneath the mounds of luggage spilling over from the passenger seat.

It's nearly six in the morning, and it's past time to go.

"The waves are crap," my brother reports when he returns.

"Good, you can surf later."

"Yeah, I'll check back in a couple hours. Maybe I should bring my board to the Shores?"

"You could," I reply. Nervous. "There will be a ton of people today, though, for the holiday."

"Oh, right. Let's get out of here before traffic."

"Let's go already!"

"Let's do it," he says, and jumps into his rusting green Explorer.

The morning is beautiful, a perfect Southern California morning with the sun shining and clear roads. The wind hits my face and plays with my ponytail as I pick up speed to merge onto Highway 5. My brother is in the rearview mirror singing along to music. Probably Tristan Prettyman, but it's hard to tell. I smile at his earnestness, brow furrowed, getting the lyrics just right. I smile at this young Navy officer who is trying so hard to be a civilian hippie surfer.

I look along the highway as we drive. I know Ben has moved into an apartment along the Five, in a canyon. This is all I know right now, and I look more at the buildings lining the highway than at the road ahead of me. If I'm not looking at the buildings alongside the Five, I'm looking at each car rushing past hoping for a glimpse of Ben's black Jeep. I know he's nearby, I just don't know where. I know I could stop my little red Fiat in the middle of the Five, get out, and easily walk to the place Ben now calls home. But would I go left or right? North or south? If I stand on the hood of my stopped Fiat and yell his name with all my might, would he hear?

It doesn't matter much, I know. With all these strangers swarming around, above, and below, I wouldn't be able to find him. Anyway, I don't dare take any of the exits in search of his black Jeep, not with my brother behind me.

"Not bad," my brother says after we pull up the driveway to my new home. I've been without a home of my own for almost two months, and I'm looking forward to a sense of independence. This little cottage isn't great, but it's providing a chance to create my own space again, so I agree with my brother.

"Nope, not bad at all."

The cottage is wide open, the French doors in front swung out, inviting us in. It's nestled in the corner of a large property behind a main house at the end of a long driveway. The ocean is close enough to hear the life-guard announcements, and soon the street in front of the main house will be full of beachgoers' cars from all over San Diego.

The cottage is small: just three rooms and a bath-room. I have work to do here, though. All of the rooms could use a cleaning. I begin thinking of things I should get at Target: bathmat, picture frames, sham-poo for Ben, sheets, doormat, air freshener. All of the windows and doors are open and Bugsy, the dog who comes with the cottage, has greeted us at the threshold.

I worry a little about Bugsy. I've never known an animal to like Ben, and in our history together, pets have never been happy in our home. I try not to worry, as Bugsy is a very easygoing, happy dog. Maybe this will be the dog to be Ben's best friend. Maybe this dog will be the one to do what all the others couldn't.

"Where do you want this?"

My brother has been busy unloading the cars as I poke around the corners and cabinets of my new home.

"Anywhere, I'll spend time unpacking later."

"You sure? I'm here, I can do whatever."

"Yeah, thanks, I want to get to Target first thing."

"Okay," he shrugs.

I know he's probably ready to get back to his house and jump in the water. This is good. Everything is working out perfectly. I can be to Target by eight, and I know my brother won't want to leave Ocean Beach once he gets back so he doesn't lose his parking spot. If Ben calls, I'll be ready. I'll be alone. I'll have a home waiting for him.

"That's it," my brother says, setting down a potted plant. "Is there anything left?"

"Nope, that's everything."

"Not bad, I'm really impressed."

"The garage sale helped."

"Oh yeah, that would do it."

There's awkwardness here, and I know he knows I'm hiding something. This makes me nervous.

"Well, thanks so much," I start.

"Yeah, sure. What are you up to the rest of the day?"

"You know, Target, unpacking, making this place like home."

"Sure, well, we're having a fire on the beach tonight, fireworks, the whole deal. You should come on by."

"Maybe," I smile. "We'll see how this goes."

I stand in front of the open French doors and wave as my brother backs out of the long driveway. Waving back when he reaches the end, he pulls into the street, and I can see the traffic is already starting to build. I stand and wave as long as he's in front of me, the little red Fiat parked just on the other side of the gate between him and me. As soon as he is gone I turn to the cottage, taking inventory of everything I see between the French doors and the bathroom.

The first issue is the stench. Bugsy smells like an outdoor dog, but he's inside with me right now. Looking down at his round, yellow, stinking body, I'm glad at the decision to leave Huey with my mom's parents, Ma and Papa, who live nearby. Two dogs in this small space would be too much for Ben. Huey and Ben have had a tumultuous relationship, anyway, and as the months have passed with them apart, I hope for the day when Huey won't remember Ben and they can start over. Today isn't the day, though. Today, I must make a home for myself and for Ben with what little we have left from the last five years together.

Target isn't even open yet when I get there, but a small crowd has formed outside the door, and I decide to join them. I know exactly what I need, and where I need to go to get it, and in what order I'm shopping. I go over my list as I wait in front of Target's closed doors.

After Target is the grocery store, for a little food and sunflowers. We had sunflowers at our wedding. They were all over my parents' backyard. It's the state flower of Kansas, where we met. I want to be sure to have a little piece of home and familiarity in our cottage. I want to be sure there are sunflowers. There is a book to get after groceries about surviving infidelity in a marriage, and I want to be sure it is there at the cottage, too. I already know I will casually place it beside the sunflowers on the table, with the other books like it that I've picked up over the last few months.

Inside the store, a red-clad employee is walking head down toward the crowd, keys in hand, and the people around me rise and shift in anticipation. I have already taken a look around the crowd for a woman about my age. She would be petite, I think, and I think with brown hair. But I'm not sure. Right now all I know is that she has a daughter, works with my husband, and she has shared a bed with him. I don't let myself consider the possibility of what I might also know. That she might also live in an apartment off the Five, in a canyon.

That doesn't matter, though, because today Ben will probably call wanting to share a home again with me. I have no real reason to think he is living with this stranger, other than his confession a month ago that he had slept with her, something he later denied. I just know he has a roommate and wants out. He wants to be at the cottage with me.

I breeze past the jumble of people vying for carts at the entrance and make my way toward the back of the store. I know exactly what I need. The sheets are on the very back wall, and I pause for a moment to consider whether to get pink or white. If Ben doesn't call, I would want the pink for myself. If he does call, white would be a far better choice.

"Screw him!" I think to myself, and grab the pink. After the last few months, he can suffer to sleep on pink sheets. The only other hiccup in my shopping is trying to find Ben's shampoo. It's always hiding in a new spot, and Ben mentioned a week or so ago that he hadn't been able to find it. I was going to, so his shampoo would be waiting for him in the shower at the cottage. Another piece of home. Finding it on the bottom shelf, I stand up and place the bottle on top of the pink sheets and stop.

Something isn't quite right here.

"Can I help you find something?" His nametag says Ted, and I know he is responding to my puzzled face.

"Oh no, thank you, I've got it all, actually."

"Well let me know if I can be of help."

"Sure, Ted. Thanks."

My thoughts no longer safe in this aisle with Ted and his good intentions, I start toward the checkout, balancing all the items on the list in my arms.

The pink sheets just aren't right.

"Screw him," I say again to myself. "You want pink, so get pink. He might not even call."

Walking to my little red Fiat with the sun slowly rising above, heating the black pavement beneath my feet, the pink sheets hit my leg as the big white bag swings from my arm. I already know I'll be back later to exchange them for white. I already know Ben will call.

The sunflowers are on sale, a good omen. With the plastic surrounding them crackling in the wind, I pull into the bookstore parking lot, the only car around. They don't open until ten. Without the time to sit and wait, I know I can come tomorrow while Ben is at work.

Gripping the steering wheel tightly, I work to turn the car, wishing for power steering. As the red Fiat reverses its course, my arms slightly throbbing from the effort, my phone rings.

"Husband," the caller ID reads, flashing a picture of Ben from the very first day we bought our phones back in Kansas. We had taken pictures of each other sitting in the Sonic parking lot, waiting for our food. I love this picture of his smiling face, the Sonic Menu a halo around his head.

I smile at the picture. I knew he would call.

"What's up? How's it going?" he asks.

"Good. Just getting all moved in."

"Is there room in the driveway for my Jeep?"

My heart skips a beat.

"Yes, there's plenty of room."

"Did you check to see if storage is open?"

"Yes, it's open all day until five. I can meet you there."

"Okay, good."

"Good."

"Are you sure about this?" he asks.

"You're more than welcome at the cottage, Ben."

"I know, but are you sure you don't want to just date for a while, you in your house, me in mine?"

"I want to be with you, Ben. It's that simple."

"Yeah, until you kick me out."

"I'm not going to kick you out," I say gently.

"You might."

"I won't."

"You said yesterday you wanted me to move slowly." Suddenly he is accusatory. Sarcastic.

"I do. You said you have a terrible living situation, and I want you to be sure you aren't just making a move to get away from something."

"Well, it is a bad living situation. It's not good." He is quiet. "But I want to be with you."

"Okay," I say. This is enough for me.

"Well, I'll call when I'm at storage if you can meet me with the keys."

"Sure, do you need help moving out?"

"No. Thanks, though. Is there anything we need at the cottage? Bookshelves?"

"Nope."

"Dresser?"

"Nope."

"Stereo?"

"Nope, it's all there."

"Well, good, because that's all I've got. You sold all our stuff," he says, and I can feel the giant finger of the universe pointing to me in fault.

"You said you didn't want any of it!"

"I know, but I still can't believe you sold all our stuff."

"You were there, Ben, you could have stopped it."

"Are you sure about this?" he asks again.

"Yes," I reply. "My home will always be open to you."

"Okay, well. I'll call in a bit."

"Okay. Talk to you soon."

I look around the Fiat. Sunflowers? Check. Target supplies? Check. Groceries? Check. Just missing the book, but we might not need it, anyway.

Ben is moving out of his apartment just off the Five, in the canyon. Tonight he'll be with me, in a cottage by the ocean, in clean white sheets that I'll race back to Target to get in exchange for the pink ones.

Tonight I will hold him like I used to, watching as his face slowly droops in sleep, and wonder again what happens behind his closed, fluttering eyelids.

The morning passes without a phone call. I wonder if I should just go home to the cottage and wait. The storage unit is on the Five, about ten minutes away. When he calls, it won't be far to go, but I don't want him to have to wait. I want today to go as smoothly as possible.

Finally, he calls. Driving down the stretch of alley toward our storage unit, I can see Ben's black Jeep bursting with things he claimed as his when he moved out the last time. He's smiling.

"Hey!" I call, smiling back. It's so good to see him. "Follow me."

We pass through the gate and pull into the parking

lot side by side. We're the only ones moving today, and I run to get him the biggest cart they have.

"I never thought you'd call," I tease, pulling a cart along behind me.

He shrugs, with a smile. "You know."

We hold each other, and he's there again, fitting perfectly into me. My hand goes down the back of his head to his neck, and he buries his face in my shoulder. I can feel his wedding ring as he moves his hand up and down my arm.

He's come back to me.

The first load of his things goes quickly. Opening the door to our storage unit, we laugh about how strange it is to see our whole life together, packed tightly into a five-by-ten space. Piled high are things that once were at home with us in Kansas, then Missouri, then on Park Boulevard just miles away. Now they sit here, perched and pressed against one another. A few units down, toward the window at the end of the narrow hall, is another five-by-ten space filled to the brim with our wedding presents, stacked neatly away, waiting to be unwrapped.

"Do you need help packing on the other end?" I ask.

"No, I've got a handle on it."

"Okay. Can I bring you lunch?"

"No, I'll grab a bite to eat."

"Okay. Well, good luck. Let me know if I can help."

"Sure."

I give him directions to the cottage. This seals our deal. Now Ben knows where I live. I still don't know where he has been living, but now it doesn't matter. He'll be home tonight. I rush back to the cottage to clean and prepare for Ben's arrival.

By the time his Jeep pulls up the driveway to park behind the red Fiat, the entire cottage sparkles. I've washed the white sheets, and with the blue and green pillows I pulled from storage while I was there, the smallish bed looks cozy in the tiny bedroom.

The air freshener has been working all afternoon, and Bugsy has been ordered repeatedly outside, where he sits happily until the slam of Ben's Jeep door. Once again, the Jeep is piled full of Ben's things. His guitar. His clothes. Our computer. It frames Ben as he pauses to look up where I'm standing in the French doors of the small white building. He smiles. I wave.

Bugsy rushes to the gate to see who has come.

Please, please like Ben, I think. Please Bugsy, like him.

Coming through the gate, Ben bends to pat Bugsy's head. Satisfied and unaffected, Bugsy returns to his place in the backyard, under the tree.

"So this is it," Ben says.

"Yup. Welcome home."

Ben smiles. A half-smile. His eyes are worried.

He doesn't like it, I think.

I follow him through the open French doors to the main part of the cottage and watch as he sits down. I sit down across from him and smile.

"Disappointed?" I ask.

"It's pretty small," he says. "But no."

I don't know what to say, and find myself looking around at something to fix. Maybe there is something here I can fix.

"You know, it's funny," Ben starts, "but as soon as I pulled up, I wondered why I was here."

My heart sinks, and I wait.

"You've never answered a question."

"What's that?"

"Why should I stay," he states. He doesn't ask.

"Why should you stay?" I'm incredulous. "Don't you think that's more of a question I should be asking you?"

"No, I'm serious. Why should I stay?"

"Because we're married. Because we promised each other for better and worse."

Ben is shaking his head.

"Because we've been through too much together

not to at least try. We have to at least try."

"Those are all your reasons why I should stay. What are my reasons for why I should stay? If you can't answer this, then that's saying something right there."

His eyes are piercing, but somehow I see them as lost. I want to give him the answer he's looking for, but I can't think of it.

"I'll think about it, Ben." I am earnest. "I'll think about it and get back to you."

There's silence, and I curse myself for not having the answer. The answer isn't in the room, and there's nothing in the room I can fix to make this better. I look at my husband and think, I love you. But I can't say it out loud. He might roll his eyes like he did last time I said it, and I can't see that right now.

"Do you have plans tonight?" he asks.

"Nope."

"Nothing with your aunt and uncle, or brother?"

"Nope."

"That's sad," he says.

"Do you have plans?" I ask, wanting to be pleasing, to be pleasant.

"I could call around and see what's going on, but no."

We look at each other.

"Are you hungry?" he asks.

I nod.

"What are you thinking?"

"How about pizza," I suggest, and he agrees.

We unload his Jeep, piling all of his belongings into the front room of the cottage to be sorted later. Opening the Jeep door, I slide into the seat where I've belonged for so long. I bought him this Jeep, and I have always loved settling in beside him, wind rushing past us, my feet reaching for the heat that hisses and spurts out the floor panel. I feel like I'm home. We go to a pizza place close to where we used to live, a place we frequented thanks to my aunt and uncle, who live nearby.

When Ben first stopped coming home, before I knew of the girl, I moved to this neighborhood and into my aunt and uncle's home. After dinner, Ben asks if I want to drive by their house, and I say no, let's just keep it you and me for a while. He agrees, quickly.

In order to avoid passing their house on the way home, Ben expertly takes a turn here, and then a turn there, one more turn, and suddenly we're on the other side of my aunt and uncle's house, looking up at their corner.

"See," Ben points out, "you can see them, but they can't see you."

"Wow," I say. I don't know what else to say. "Cool."

"Yeah." He's proud of himself.

I know from his dancing eyes that this isn't the

first time he's taken those turns and ended up stopped like this, looking up at their house.

"I always knew where you were. Every night, I knew," he says.

I don't know what to say, so I smile.

We decide to stop at Target. Ben wants a blanket for our bed.

"You didn't think we'd just sleep with a sheet, did you?" he had asked when he saw the bed I had made with white sheets and blue and green pillows.

"It's July," I shrugged.

"No," he said simply.

We are at Target, the one I opened this morning, debating about which blanket to get. We decide on a blue and green one to match the pillows, and he pulls me close with a smile. It's as though nothing strange has happened. We're here at Target, deciding what will work best in our home. We've done this before, practically every year we've been together. Building a home.

We get in the Jeep to go to the cottage, and at this point in the night, I'm no longer wondering where Ben woke up this morning. It doesn't matter.

Driving along the Five, north to our cottage, fireworks are bursting all around in the dark night sky.

"There, look at that!" I point.

"Where?" Ben leans forward and looks up, but he's missed them.

"I'll keep looking."

I turn in my seat to watch the fireworks going off behind the hill we're speeding away from.

"You're missing it," I say to Ben.

"Oh well."

He doesn't care.

When we get to the cottage we try to look over the shrubs surrounding the property to see the fireworks splashing the darkened sky. We're too late though and turn to go inside.

"I figured I could learn how to play the guitar while we're here," Ben says, carrying his case to the chair in the living room. I bought him the guitar, a nice one, two years ago. I'm glad he's thought of it to fill the time without a television or other distraction. I make a note in my head to find a guitar teacher in the neighborhood so I can surprise Ben with lessons. I'm not working now, and I'll have the time to do such searches.

We pull out the chessboard for a quick game, and he takes my king in less than a dozen moves.

"You need to pay more attention," he says.

I agree.

Soon it's bedtime and we're brushing our teeth,

doing a dance around each other and the sink as we have for the last five years. Ben asks a question, his mouth full of toothpaste, and I laugh as he tries to keep everything in his mouth. He smiles.

In bed, the light from the moon is shining down on us through the window.

"Good night," I whisper.

The darkness is still.

"I love you," I whisper.

The room is still.

I hold Ben, and my heart is full feeling the familiar curves of his body next to mine.

"That's way too bright," he says, turning into me, pushing me backward into the pillow.

"I've got it," I say, jumping up. "Stay where you are."

Pulling the curtains closed, I lay back down beside Ben, bringing the white sheets up to my chin, the blue and green blanket around my shoulders.

The door creaks open. I can smell Bugsy before I see him.

"No!" Ben barks, lifting his head.

"I've got it." I jump up. "Bugsy, no."

Gently pushing his wet nose into the living room, I quietly shut the door and ease my hand off the knob.

"The fan is humming. Do you hear that?"

I have sold the nice, expensive fan I bought Ben

for his birthday at our garage sale, and this cheap little black fan came from Target this morning. I made a third, special trip to get it when I remembered that Ben needs a fan to sleep. I wish for the expensive, shining silver fan to be here instead of this little black piece of plastic.

"Is this better?" I ask, turning the fan on its side.

"No. Just leave it."

"Maybe if I—"

"Leave it," Ben interrupts.

Defeated, I climb over Ben to my side of the bed against the wall and lay on my back watching the shadows on the ceiling. My cell phone blinks red with a message on the dresser, and I slowly turn my head to see if Ben will notice the small flash. My family has been calling all day, but the phone is on silent so it wouldn't interrupt. So I wouldn't have to explain.

After a while, I know I should turn to Ben and hold him, and be glad to have him so close. For the first time in months, I know where he's sleeping. For the first time in months, I know who he's sleeping beside. I watch as his breathing slows, and I try not to let the tears rolling down my cheek to the pillow make a sound when they land.

"Good night. I love you," I mouth to the back of his head and close my eyes, hoping for sleep.

3

WEDNESDAY

I don't call him during the day while he's working. I never did that often. When I did, he was busy. Rushed. I hated hearing "Why are you calling?" so I didn't. Today I decide I won't call because I don't want to say the wrong thing, and I want him to come home.

He wakes up early, and while he is in the shower I hurry Bugsy to the ocean for his morning walk. I know that if I can get Bugsy walked before he sees Ben, he'll be a good dog. This is what I want, for Bugsy to be a good dog. For Ben to come home.

The waves are low, and the surfers sit on the surface of water, waiting. Bugsy wants to stop and sniff, but I don't let him. Ben is home, getting ready for work, and I want to be there to say goodbye. Pulling Bugsy behind me I make it to the driveway and am relieved to see Ben's Jeep is still there.

"Good morning!" I smile, coming through the open French doors, careful not to be too cheery but just cheery enough.

"Morning," Ben responds as he walks by me to the bedroom.

He hasn't unpacked and is digging in his suitcase for a clean shirt.

"Need help?" I offer.

"Yes. Find a clean shirt, will you? And a white undershirt."

"Sure," and I kneel to sort through the familiar shirts while he goes back to the bathroom to shave. Pulling out a favorite shirt of mine and a clean white undershirt, I carefully place them on the bed.

The bed should be made, I think, and I jump up to do it before the buzz of Ben's razor stops.

"Not that one." He's in the door. "It's going to be ninety degrees inland. Something cooler."

"Right," I say and return to his suitcase.

"That one will work," he says. I have a shirt in each hand and look at him for clarity.

"This one?" I ask, holding up my left hand.

"No, that one," he says, and I gently place the shirt he's chosen next to the undershirt at the end of the made bed.

"Can I get you breakfast?" I ask. I've made muesli

just for Ben with the soymilk he likes. It's waiting in the fridge for him to say yes.

"Sure. What do you have?"

"Cereal I made fresh yesterday. Do you want to try it?"

He shrugs. I spoon the cereal into a bowl for him.

"That's too much," he says, and I spoon some back into the mixing bowl.

"Little more," he says, and I spoon some back into his bowl.

He sits to eat. I try to find a way to be natural sitting across from him.

"What are you doing today?" he asks.

"Job search, cleaning up messes here and there, walking the dog, you know."

He keeps eating.

"Do you want me to wait for you to walk Bugsy tonight?"

"Whatever," Ben says.

"I'll give you a call, how 'bout?"

He shrugs and is finished eating.

I stand and he kisses me goodbye, and I'm happy seeing that he has his wedding ring on.

"Have a good day," I smile.

"I will. You, too."

I follow him out to the front of the cottage and watch

as he gets in his Jeep. I wave until he reaches the end of the driveway and turns, disappearing into the traffic.

If I don't hurry I'll be late for daily mass, and I want to be sure I cover all my bases. I want to be sure to thank God for answering my constant prayer to bring Ben back to me. He did. Ben is here. Ben will be home again tonight.

Moving quickly, I know what I'll look like in this fancy neighborhood showing up for morning mass in shorts and flip-flops, but I don't care.

Sitting in the back pew, I can barely contain myself. There is something buzzing inside me that wants to move and is pained to sit still. But I must cover this base. I know I need all the help I can get. I'm starting to feel that between Ben and me maybe I am the crazy one, not him. I'm starting to feel that all of this is my fault. I'm starting to feel that I'm losing control. But this is my husband. This is a marriage. There is something, somewhere, that can fix this. I'm at church. I'm covering this base.

I can't understand the priest. He's visiting from Scotland, and his accent is more than I can process. I'm left with my thoughts. I'm wishing I had picked out the right shirt this morning, and I'm crushed that I didn't. I know this means something is wrong. Something is terribly wrong. Something is wrong with me.

Ben will be home tonight, though, and I shouldn't be bothered with things that aren't right with me. I've always been the strong one—it's my job to take care of us. I must find a way to take care of us.

I leave mass before the service is over, pushing through the heavy wooden doors to a sun-filled, empty street. It's still the early morning hours, and I know I should visit Ma and Papa just a few blocks away.

Huey is beside himself when he sees me, his little body wiggling and shaking at my feet. My grandparents are still in their pajamas. They've lived here in this white house in La Jolla since my mom was in high school. We chat, and I go to the backdoor to let Huey out. There is a stretch of dirt in their backyard where a deck used to be. Before things started happening Ben had helped Papa tear the deck out with plans to rebuild a new one. Then things started happening.

"We're getting far on the new deck," Papa jokes, behind me.

"Yeah, looks good," I smile. I feel guilty because Ben was supposed to help with the new deck, but all he's done is take the old one out, leaving this mess.

"Let's go sit outside," Papa says.

I don't want to but do because I know I won't be back until Sunday. Ben doesn't work on Fridays or Saturdays, so I won't come then. Tomorrow I'm spending the day trying to get into art school. Now is my chance to see them, to see Huey.

Huey is happy and full of energy. It's good to see him so full of life. I was at work when he had an accident that broke one leg in three places and broke the other leg at the hip two years ago. Ben was the only one home so I think Huey associated that pain with him. Without Ben around, Huey has been acting like a puppy again. He and our cat, Captain Jack, came here when things started happening. As the weeks wore on here with my grandparents, Captain Jack started becoming adventurous. He is outside with us now, basking in the sun.

"He still won't let men touch him, but he's doing great with Ma," Papa says.

"That's fantastic!" I say, and mean it.

"Yes. He doesn't run out of the room anymore when I come into it, which is good progress."

"That's really good," I say, and try to sound energetic. "Thanks so much for taking care of them."

I leave them, and Huey watches as I drive down the block. I wave the whole way until I reach the corner. It's a relief to be free from the confines of conversation. It's hard to concentrate on any line of thought that isn't related to Ben and how I can fix us.

Going down the hill from my grandparents' house to the ocean, I pull to the side of the street under a large tree and stop. Down stairs that twist twice then open onto huge boulders that meet the sea, I find a spot to sit and watch the ocean.

I ask for peace. I ask for strength. I ask for endurance. I ask for wisdom. I ask God to help Ben. I ask God to please help me. I ask him to please bring my Ben back to me.

I spend the rest of the day waiting.

I should be looking for a job, but I can't sit still.

I'm waiting.

Ben calls, but I don't answer. I'm afraid of what I might say. Then Ben doesn't call, and I want to call him to see if he wants to walk Bugsy with me, but I don't.

And then, I do.

"I don't know," he says when I ask. "I don't know how late I'll be here—go if you need to go."

"I don't need to go but wanted to invite you along if you wanted to."

"Just do what you need to do," he says, and so I take Bugsy and we walk for an hour along the beach.

When I hear Ben's Jeep turn into the driveway, I look around. The rug is straight and centered. The dishes are done. The bathroom is fresh, the towels are hanging perfectly. The bed is made and pillows adjusted exactly as he likes them: sideways, balancing on a corner like diamonds. Everything is perfect, and I go outside to meet him.

"Hey!" I smile. I have just showered, and put on a cute new skirt and top, and feel ready to deal with Ben. Everything is perfect.

"Grab your keys," he says from the other side of the gate, and I rush inside to get them. Grabbing something to tie my hair back with, I run through the cottage and meet Ben just outside the open French doors. I hug him.

"How was your day?" I ask.

"Fine," he says. He always says fine. For five years the only thing he says about his days are that they are fine. Instead of annoying me, like it used to, I smile at his response. My Ben is back.

"Let's go, are you ready?"

"Yup," I smile, and hold out the keys to my little red convertible. "You can drive."

We get in the car, and at the end of the driveway, Ben asks which way we should go.

"North." The answer is simple.

His apartment off the Five, in a canyon, and our old apartment on Park Boulevard are all south. North is the way to go. We drive, the warm summer air rushing past us, and I smile. I'm happy, I think.

"What's this?" Ben asks, pointing to a knob on the dashboard.

"Haven't figured it out yet," I say, smiling.

Ben is playing with the knob as we round a corner.

"Whoa, stay on your side of the road," he says to me, looking up in time to correct the path of the car. On our right is a deep canyon, nothing but a thin guardrail between it and us.

"Wouldn't be good," Ben says, looking over the rail.

"Would solve a lot of our problems, though," I joke.

Ben looks at me, straight-faced. "What problems?"

"Oh, I don't know." I try to recover, and look away.

The sun is slowly setting, and in front of us is a winding road, leading down to a large stretch of beautiful, sparkling beach. We're headed north on Highway 1. This is a moment like the kind we talked about sitting in our small, cold apartment in Kansas City no more than a year before.

I look over at Ben. Behind him the world is glowing blue and golden, the clouds shocks of white in an otherwise clear sky.

My cell phone flashes red. I look long enough to see my brother is calling before easing it down the side of my seat, out of sight. Ben doesn't see any of this. I want to enjoy this moment.

We keep driving until we reach a small town along the highway with stop signs at every corner, and we decide to turn around and go home for dinner. As we pass by quaint little restaurants I tell Ben it would be fun to drive back up sometime for dinner or brunch. He smiles and raises his eyebrows but doesn't respond.

The air is diffusing into a chill and my body shivers to keep warm. I try to hide this. Ben hates it when I'm cold, and I'm angry with myself for shivering.

"Are you cold?" he asks, noticing. "How can you be cold?"

"Dunno. Just am," I smile and try harder to relax.

"Which of these is the heat?" he asks, and he's back to playing with the dashboard.

"I haven't had to use it yet, I'm not sure. I'm okay, though, Ben, really. It's not that cold, we're almost home."

We pull back into our driveway, squeezing past Ben's Jeep parked just off to the side so the Fiat is closest to the cottage.

Just a block or two away is a road packed with restaurants, and I take Ben's hand for the walk to dinner. It's familiar, this hand, and I hold on tighter as we cross the street.

"I've missed you," I say when we're on the other side

and look up to him as we walk. He smiles and watches the sidewalk.

"I'm so sorry," I say.

"For what?"

"I started this."

"No, you didn't," he says, shaking his head. "I did."

"I could've done things so much better, though," I say. "There's a lot I regret."

"You've always been a good friend, Jamie."

"Hmm." I want the conversation to end. "Thanks."

I don't want him to ask again if I know why he should stay, because I still don't have his answer. I change the topic from us to cars. I manage to have endless questions about my 1969 Fiat.

We find a hamburger joint still open and place our orders before running next door to the beach market for cash. Ben goes inside to pay, and I snag one of the tables for us out front. We share a meal like we have for five years. Casually. Easily. It's just us again. I love that we're here. I love that we have our wedding rings on.

"Do you want ice cream?"

"Sure," I say, and I let him pick the flavor for us to share. He takes the first bite and tells me I'll hate it, and he's right, I do. But I don't say so. Walking slowly, passing the ice cream back and forth between us, we move toward the ocean, now a black void a block away.

The tide is high, and I can hear the waves crashing between the words Ben and I say to each other. We're walking into the wind, and the smell of the salt water is thick. Ben stands in front of the seawall, waiting for me to return from throwing away our ice cream cup. As I walk, I look up to the sky and quietly thank God. Thank him for answering my prayers.

Ben is in front of me now, hands in pockets, and I ask him how warm he thinks the water is. He shrugs. Kicking off my flip-flops, I run to the water and sink my feet into wet sand. The water is cold and I shriek. Running back to Ben, I sit on the wall looking up at him, wiping the sand from my feet. He's just standing there, looking out to the ocean. The moon is out and dancing white on the waves. The beach is ours.

I stand up and put my arms around Ben's waist and pull myself close to him. I hold him like this for a while, until I know he isn't going to relax his body or take his hands from his pockets to hold me, too. I ease away from him. It's time to go.

"We should go walk Bugsy," he says.

"Oh, I took care of it," I reply.

"You didn't wait for me?"

"I'm sorry."

"You didn't call."

"I'm sorry."

"Doesn't matter."

We walk back to the cottage, and I ask him if he believes in creating your own destiny or if he believes it's all predetermined. God's will or free will. It's something I've been wondering a lot about lately and think maybe Ben's answer will work for mine, too. Free will, he says. No discussion.

I'm not satisfied.

We turn down our driveway to see the old man from the main house shining a flashlight into our black Jeep. Ben and I smile at each other.

The old man looks up at us, turning the flashlight off quickly.

"Hello!" Ben says. I've always loved how charming Ben can be. "How are you?" he asks.

"Fine, fine," the old man replies.

"We haven't met yet. We're staying in your cottage for a little while." Ben extends his hand. The old man takes it.

"I'm Ben, and this is my wife, Jamie."

I smile and shake the old man's hand. "Good to meet you."

"Who are you?" the old man asks.

"This is my wife, Jamie," Ben replies, "and I'm Ben, her husband."

The old man smiles. I can see he's embarrassed.

"You're in the cottage?"

We smile.

"These are your cars?"

We smile.

"Nice to meet you," Ben says, and with perfect coordination we both turn to go inside.

Walking through the gate, Ben and I smile at each other.

The chessboard comes out, and we play two games. Ben beats me at both. Unlike last night, tonight I put up a good fight, and we laugh at our seriousness when we're finished.

While Ben brushes his teeth, I make sure the curtain in the bedroom is closed so the moon won't shine in, I send Bugsy outside, I put the little black plastic fan on its side so it won't hum.

Crawling into bed, I wait for Ben to follow. When he does, he gently pulls the sheets down, careful to keep me covered. Taking his glasses off and placing them on the bedside table, he turns the light off and settles into his pillow.

As I lay there watching the darkness, Ben turns, his arm gently sliding over my stomach to pull me close.

Like I had for countless nights before, I gently put my hand on his elbow and move slowly up his arm to his hand. I fold my hands over his, and hold it there. Both of my hands and his, just under my chin. Just as it should be. Just as it has been. My Ben came back to me. Thank you, God. Thank you.

4

THURSDAY

I want this morning to go as smoothly as yesterday morning did, so I get up again when I hear the shower start. If I time it just right I can get Bugsy to the beach and back before Ben is dressed for work. Ben still hasn't mentioned the special shampoo I found for him, and I wonder if he hasn't yet seen it sitting on the floor of the shower. I think for a second of calling in to tell him the shampoo is there but then decide this is silly and grab Bugsy's leash instead.

The beach is full this morning. The waves are good. I stop for a moment and look out at the ocean and am careful to think of how lucky I am to live here. Scripps Pier is in the distance in one direction, La Jolla Cove the other. It's beautiful. The air is still and the smell of the ocean mixes and mingles with the scent of the flowers in the park to my left. Bugsy is satisfied, and

I feel happy thinking of Ben two blocks away. I know exactly where he is, and I'm suddenly anxious to see his face. We run, Bugsy and I, back toward the cottage. I'm relieved again to see the black Jeep, still where it was from the night before.

Ben is in the bathroom, and I expertly dish just the right amount of cereal for him. Not too much, not too little. So it will keep chilled, I put the bowl of cereal in the fridge and I go to see if I can pick out a shirt for Ben.

"I've already done that," he says from the doorway. I turn, and he's already dressed.

"So you have," I smile and reach to zip his suitcase.

"I could use some socks, though. They might be in the laundry basket in the closet."

"Sure," I say. "Do you want breakfast?"

"Maybe," Ben calls from the main room.

"There's a bowl of cereal for you in the fridge!" I call from the closet, where I'm focused on finding a pair of brown dress socks for Ben to wear today.

I find them, and Ben is sitting down eating.

"Tonight's softball," he says between spoonfuls.

"Oh, believe me, I know," I joke.

"You know I'm going, right?"

"I want you to go. I think you should."

"I don't even think she'll be there."

"Okay," I say, trying not to care.

"There are some things I need you to do today."

"Sure."

He stands up and goes to the desk to write his list. He hates the generic dish soap that's here. If there's one thing he hates, it's generic dish soap, so I'm to get something better than what we have. The lotion I have bought is too girlie (it has sparkles) so he would like normal lotion, please. Food, maybe frozen pizza for dinner tonight. Something easy, because he has a game at nine. Cancel the electricity from our old apartment on Park Boulevard in Hillcrest. Be sure, also, that the cable has been cancelled. Call our landlord to see if we're getting our deposit back. Call to see if our laptop can be fixed. That's it.

I do everything on the list, except one. I go to Target and I get apple-scented dish soap, and no-scent, no-sparkle lotion. Old Navy is next to Target, so I stop to get Ben new khakis. It's not on the list, but he's complained the last two days about the pair he's been wearing being too big, so I guess at a size, grab a Hawaiian shirt I think he'll like, and keep moving. At the grocery store I get frozen pizza and Ben's favorite snacks, and at the checkout I see an advertisement for guitar lessons nearby. Perfect. I take down the information.

I make phone calls when I get home. The electricity at our old apartment was cancelled automatically a week ago when the new tenant moved in, as was the cable. Our deposit is on its way to our new P.O. box. Perfect.

I have just enough time now to get downtown for my admissions interview at an art school.

I feel like I fit in here at the art school. My nose is pierced now, and I feel like it makes me look like an art student and not a Midwestern, Catholic schoolgirl. I've always drawn, always created little projects or made my own clothes. This strange turn of events is providing the opportunity for me to become who I really am, I think. Maybe this pierced-nose, art-student gig is who I really am.

I take the tour, meet with an admissions counselor, and am told that because of my high level of education it will be easier for me to be admitted. I could start classes in just one week. I'm excited as I run back to the car.

Today, I have driven our car downtown. My car and Ben's, the one we've shared the last four years. It's a blue Volkswagen Golf I've envisioned gently placing our newborns into as we bring each home from the hospital. Sometimes Ben and I would joke in this car about our future family and laugh as we say to the

empty back seat, "Nigel, quiet, no we aren't there yet."
We had already named our children, making it even
easier to imagine them tucked carefully into the backseat of this little blue car. Nigel. Owen. These names
were my idea, and Ben loved them.

While I was inside the art school trying on a
new life a street cleaner passed, leaving dark brown
splashes on an otherwise sparkling car. I sigh heavily
when I see this. One more thing to add to the list. Must
clean the Golf.

I get in the car and call Ben at work. I'm excited.
He has time to talk, and I get to really share how happy
I am. Things are getting so much better between us, I
think, as I hang up. Things are good.

I stop in Ocean Beach on the way home and spend
a little more than an hour driving around looking for
available apartments. I stop the car every time I see a
sign and take down the number and address. We only
have the cottage for another month, then we'll need
something else. I get more than a dozen phone numbers, with details of who to call and where they're
located. I try to think of everything Ben will ask
because I want to be sure to have the answers. I want
him to be impressed with my thoroughness. Ben likes
windows, open spaces, and good light. Ben likes to be
near the water. I haven't found the perfect apartment

yet, but I've put in a good effort. I tuck my notes carefully away and start the drive home to the cottage in La Jolla Shores. Driving through Ocean Beach to go north I pass my brother's house, but I don't stop. There would be questions, and I don't have answers.

I'll be home in time to get everything in order before Ben gets home, and I roll all the windows down as I make my way up the Five. I don't have to bother looking for Ben's Jeep. I know where it is. I don't have to bother inspecting buildings alongside the highway. I know where Ben lives.

Everything is ready for him. The rug is perfectly centered. The bed is made. The towels hang perfectly. I think Ben will be home in about forty minutes so I change into my bathing suit, fit the rash guard over my head, and grab my surfboard for the walk to the beach. I've never done this by myself before, and the board is heavy. I'm a beginner, so the board is made of thick foam, and I can just barely fit it under my arm. A block from the cottage I put the board on my head and balance it the rest of the way to the beach. There are a lot of people on the beach. I know I'll be watched, this small blond girl with a big red surfboard. I know I won't get up. I also know I want Ben to see that I'm changing. That I'm fun. That I'm not afraid of trying new things.

I find a space between groups of surfers and paddle out a few hundred feet from shore. I don't really want to be surfing. I really just want Ben to see me walking home with the board. I let a few waves send me reeling under water, groping and twisting for my board before I go back to dry land. Good enough, I think.

Finding my sandals on the beach, I lift the big red board to my head and walk the few blocks home. I walk slowly partly because I'm tired, and partly because it would be absolutely ideal if Ben were to see me walking home. This is the plan. I turn the corner to the drive-way and am disappointed to see only my little red Fiat. I've been parking the blue Golf around the corner so it won't remind Ben of our old life together. Besides this, it's dirty now, and I want a chance to clean it before Ben sees it again.

I think for a moment of standing here like this in front of the Fiat, surfboard on my head, until Ben rounds the corner. I know this is ridiculous, though, and I make my way down the long driveway to the cottage in the back corner of the property. I'm prop-ping the surfboard up to dry when I hear Ben's Jeep. I turn to see him smiling at me, and I wave, glad to have been caught like this. Here I am, a Southern California surfer girl. His wife.

"How're the waves?"

"I didn't get up once," I say, and it's true.

"Have you been out much lately?"

"When I can." This is true, in a way, too.

I shower, and he chats with me on the other side of the door until I'm clean.

"I have pizza for dinner," I say.

"Good."

"Do you want to walk Bugsy with me before we eat?"

"You should have done that."

"Well, I didn't."

I think to myself that instead of doing a stupid surfing show for Ben that I should have just walked the dog. This would have been better. Practical.

"Sorry," I say.

"Whatever, let's go."

Ben lets me take the leash and doesn't seem to care that I let Bugsy sniff around. He doesn't seem to care that Bugsy stops here and there to lift his leg. I'm relieved that Ben isn't showing interest in these things and is letting Bugsy just be a dog. I think of Huey and I'm glad again that he isn't here with us. Ben hasn't asked about our dog or our cat, and I don't want to bring them up. It is better now, without them.

We walk toward Scripps Pier, and I ask Ben why things ended with the girl. He doesn't want to talk about it.

"I'm just curious why, or how," I say.

He doesn't want to talk about it.

We find a bench on a steep cliff overlooking the ocean and sit, watching people enjoy the beach below. I turn to him and hold his arm.

"I'm sorry."

He looks at me and smiles.

"I guess I just need to hear that you love me, and that you want to be with me. That's all."

"Well," he starts with a sigh, "I think I love you. And I want to be here with you right now, so—"

"Okay," I say. "Okay."

The view is breathtaking. I remind myself how beautiful it all is as I keep a hand on Ben's arm. My wedding ring presses between my finger and his flesh, and I'm aware of it there. It's heavy on my hand.

We walk past a group of surfers on our way back to the cottage, and Ben turns to me as soon as they pass. "What about them?"

"What?" I ask. I don't get it.

"What about one of those guys. They were all pretty cute, a surfer guy, eh?"

"No, thanks," I say. I still don't get it.

"Oh come on, I bet you'd like being with one of them."

"Nope," I say, shaking my head. I get it. "I pick you," I say.

He's quiet for a moment.

"What about beautiful Brian?" Ben asks, referring to a friend from college I'd always had a hopeless crush on. We used to laugh about this together.

"Nope," I say again. "He is beautiful, though." I try to joke and be lighthearted.

"I'm ugly," Ben says.

"No you aren't. I think you're handsome."

"I'm fat."

"Hardly," I say. I'm incredulous. He's easily lost twenty pounds over the last few months.

He is quiet.

"I picked you a long time ago, and I still pick you," I say with certainty.

This makes Ben mad, and he's quiet the rest of the way home.

It's Thursday, softball night, and I set out his jersey and his mitt for him. Ben has unpacked slowly over the last few days, and I'm glad I can open the dresser drawer and find his clothes there. I go to the kitchen to turn the oven on, and take out the frozen pizza.

"This is what you got?" Ben asks, holding up the empty box.

He's not happy with it. I jump up.

"It's supreme," I point out.

"Yeah," he laughs, "but who makes it?"

"I don't know. It's all the store had."

"Hmm," Ben says, tossing the box on the countertop.

"We could do something else," I offer.

"No, that's okay."

I curse the pizza as I bend to put it in the oven, and I can hear Ben in the bedroom inspecting what I bought today. I go to the bedroom and find him in the khakis from Old Navy.

"Do they work?" I ask, hopeful.

"Look," Ben says.

They look a little tight. Maybe a little short.

"What size do you think I am?" he asks.

"I wasn't sure, so I guessed."

"Obviously," his attention is on the pants. "And what is this?" He's pointing to the Hawaiian shirt.

"I thought it was kind of fun, and it was on sale. It's a medium. It should work."

"Hmm," Ben is smiling, but it's not a good smile. "Nice try."

Ben leaves with a kiss after dinner, and I wave as his Jeep moves down the long driveway. I hate that he's going. He knows this. He doesn't think she'll be there tonight, though. He tells me this twice.

While he's gone, I spend time trying to set up apartment tours for the next day. I think if I can get Ben to picture us in a place together long-term, that this will be a good thing. He needs something stable, steady. I manage to arrange a walk-through for the next morning in Ocean Beach. One block from the water, and it's big. Ben has always wanted to live in this neighborhood, and I smile at my accomplishment as I hang up the phone.

The phone rings, and it's Ben.

"Just wanted you to know I'm here," he says.

I smile.

"Good, I'm glad you made it."

"I think I get to pitch tonight."

"Cool! Good luck."

"Thanks, I'll call you later."

"Okay, I love you."

"Love you, too," he says and hangs up.

Things are good. Things are better. I settle in to clean the cottage, and start the sketches for my admissions package to art school. I'm sketching when my phone rings again.

"Hey, we won!" Ben's excited. He thinks they've won because he pitched, and now he has plans to pitch for all of their games. He can do this because he's captain.

"Anyway, we're going to get a celebratory drink. Nobody wanted to go, but I told them we should just go for one, so we're going. Just one, though. I'll be home soon."

I hear him breathing hard as he runs, the voices around him growing softer.

"You'll be happy to know your favorite person isn't even here," he says quietly.

"That's good," I say.

"Yes, it is. Love you."

"I love you, too." I'm sure he can hear my smile.

I go back to my sketchbook and draw a cartoon of Ben pitching. I write congratulations on the top of the page, and smile as I write a little love note on the bottom. I've given Ben enough pages like this to fill books, and I'm glad to keep adding to his collection.

My phone rings again, and it's Ben.

"Hey, wanted you to know I'm looking for the Jeep, and I'm on my way home."

"That was quick!" I'm surprised.

"Yeah, just one drink. Everyone wanted to go home."

"Cool."

"Anyway, I'll be home in about, oh I don't know, twenty minutes?"

"Great, I'll be here."

"Okie dokie. Love you."

"Love you, too," I say. "Be safe."

I get the bedroom ready, the curtains are pulled, the fan is on its side. I send Bugsy out the backdoor.

Ben is still excited when he comes home, and I hear about his game, and his pitching skills. He loves my drawing. I get a hug as thanks. Today was a good day. Such a good day. Ben holds my hand tight to his chest as sleep comes quickly for us both.

5

FRIDAY

We sleep in, which is nice. Nine-thirty is a luxury, and I roll over to watch my husband sleep. I can see from cracks in the curtains that it's a beautiful morning. A light breeze is coming through the cottage, and the world looks soft under the sunrays that are peeking in at us. Ben rolls over and opens sleepy eyes to me. I take this moment and breathe it in deeply. Ben looking at me, the warm light of the cottage, birds just outside the window singing above the buzz of the little black fan.

"Good morning," I whisper.

"Hmm." Ben smiles.

I love this.

He reaches over and moves hair away from my face before he turns to swing his legs over the side of the bed. I lay there for a moment, watching him go through the bedroom door toward the bathroom and wonder if he'll come back to bed.

The shower starts and I know I should go get Bugsy for his walk. Bugsy and I move quickly this morning, but not as quickly as yesterday. I know Ben will be there when we get back—he doesn't work today.

It's later than normal so the beach is busier, and Bugsy gets a lot of attention. I stop to let some young boys pet this big yellow dog before turning back home.

The sun is warm on my head and shoulders, and with seagulls crying in the sky above me I stop and lift my face to the clear blue sky. Finally, things are as they should be. Ben is home. He will put his wedding ring on today, and we'll look at apartments, introducing ourselves as husband and wife.

Ben is clean and happy when Bugsy and I return from the beach. It seems like things are normal, so I don't bother with offering cereal, or making the bed, or picking out shirts. Ben is happy. He sits at the desk, and I get ready to shower.

"Was the cottage dirty when you first got here?"

I look quickly to see if it is dirty now, but it isn't. Things are in their places.

"Well, I spent time cleaning," I say. Hoping this is safe.

"It looks really nice," he says. And I am relieved. I am happy. I am smiling.

"What is this?" he asks, holding up a piece of paper.

"I found you guitar lessons just a few blocks away," I smile and keep moving.

He looks at the information I wrote down before putting the piece of paper back on the desk.

"That's nice," he smiles.

"Yeah." I've done a good thing.

"Except one thing you keep forgetting."

"What's that?"

"Money," he says.

"Oh." I scrunch my nose. "Right."

"Yeah." His eyebrows are raised, and he turns around.

"Maybe someday," I say, before offering to bring him breakfast.

I spoon cereal into our blue bowls from Kansas, and Bugsy wanders into the cottage to say hello. Ben calls him over and scratches behind his ears and talks to him in a Scooby-Doo voice. Bugsy turns his head listening to Ben and I smile. This, finally, could be the dog that likes Ben.

"I haven't seen you go to work since I've been here," he says, still petting Bugsy.

This is trouble.

"Yeah, no worries, it's under control."

"Do you have a job, or don't you?"

He's making faces at Bugsy and blowing puffs of air in his face. Bugsy's big yellow tail is wagging back and forth, and I don't want this good morning to go away.

"I do," I say. This is somewhat true but not all the way true, which I know makes it a lie.

Ben doesn't have any more questions, and I keep moving. I look now and then at Ben and his new best friend. This dog actually likes him, I think.

Bugsy follows Ben all the way to the gate when we leave to go apartment hunting. The sun is still shining, and we're here, at a cottage near the beach, getting into a shiny red convertible. This is exactly what we talked about no more than a year ago in our cold apartment in Kansas City.

We rumble out into the traffic from the driveway, and I think of how we must appear to all the people we pass. We've been told we look like Barbie and Ken, and I secretly love this even though I say out loud that it's silly. Now I like to think the people we pass are thinking exactly this: that we are a perfect couple, in a perfect car, on a perfect Southern California day.

The apartment we look at is big, as promised. It is

one block from the ocean, as promised. We can afford it, and there is a pool twenty feet from our front door. There aren't a lot of windows, though, and it looks into another apartment in back that's ten feet away.

"It's small," I say of the kitchen when Ben and I break free of the landlord. "Not much space."

"Why do we need space?" he asks. He's smiling and grabs my waist. "You sold all of our stuff, remember?" He's close now, and I smile to him with a tilt of my head.

"You even sold our table," he points to where one would go in the dining room.

"You never liked that table."

"I never said that."

"Well, it's gone. We'll get a better one."

"But we already had one," he says, putting his arm around me.

I smile, and look at him. I'm searching his eyes to see if he's still happy or if he really is upset about the table.

When we finish looking we stand outside, in front of the pool, listening to the landlord explain deposits, leases, and timelines. Ben has a bankruptcy, and I want the landlord to know this upfront so I tell him we have less-than-sparkling credit and a bankruptcy between us. The landlord is hopeful it won't matter. He leaves us in front of the apartment to imagine our life here together, and as he walks away Ben pulls me close with one arm and kisses my head.

"When we get further from this mess, I'll show you where I was living," he says.

I want to see it now, but I don't say so. Instead I ask him what it's like.

"Terrible," he says, shaking his head. "Nothing I would have ever picked." He looks at me, and his eyes are dancing. He kisses my head again.

We agree this is a good option but that we should keep looking. We explore our would-be neighborhood, walking up the block to the ocean. We stop at the end of the street, which is also the end of dry land. We stand here at the top of the cliff, looking out to the deep blue water, and hold each other. The wind is rushing past us, and I shiver a little. Ben rubs my arms and holds me tighter.

"Will you be warm enough?" he asks. His face is worried.

"Yep." I smile up at him. "I have a sweater in the car."

The summer sun is above us, its heat piercing through the sharp wind in intervals. Heat is trapped between Ben and me, and I think I could stay here like this. Just stay. Till death do us part, for better or worse. For as bad as it was and could be again. Just stay.

The red Fiat is waiting down the block, and the day is still stretched before us so we turn and, hand in hand, walk inland.

The black seats of the little red Fiat burn my legs as I sink into the convertible, but the warmth is welcome and I leave my sweater in the backseat. I drive us around Ocean Beach looking for more apartments. I point out a few I saw yesterday, and then we give up. We're hungry.

Ben wants to take me to one of his new favorite restaurants, and I'm curious to see how he's been living. I know he might have been living near Ocean Beach for a while, but I am not sure. I'm excited to see where he takes us. He points me down endless back roads, turning and twisting, taking down available apartment numbers as we go. It's like he's been through these strange streets a thousand times, and he says as much with the directions he gives.

"After this street, you'll turn left and go two blocks before going right. Once you pass the gray apartments, you'll go right again, then left, and then we'll turn right onto the main road. Then stay in the right lane."

He's pleased with himself.

I'm starting to relax. He's happy. He's back. He's letting me into his secret world.

We stop next to a small Mexican restaurant, and

Ben already knows what we'll order. A burrito, it's perfect for two people, he says. Extra tortillas and one Coke for us to share. He orders like he's done this a thousand times, too.

"Come here often?" I ask.

"It's great end-of-the-night drunk food."

"I bet," I say, trying to figure out where he might have been living in the twisting and turning we did on the way here that would make this end-of-the-night food.

We take our food outside, and Ben offers to sit in the sun so I don't have to. The burrito is good. The tortillas are better, and I carefully eat as Ben points out the Blockbuster across the street.

"I've been there a lot," he says.

"Really?" I'm surprised. I mostly pictured him out. I didn't even think he had a television.

"What movies did you watch?"

He doesn't want to answer and keeps eating. He wants to talk more about this little hut of a restaurant we're sitting outside of.

"I came here a lot while you were gone," he says.

I don't take issue with his saying I was gone. I don't point out that I was home in our apartment on Park Boulevard waiting for him while he was here eating burritos.

"I was in the hospital for a week, and I ate here a lot after that."

"You were in the hospital?" I stop eating.

"They called you. The nurses called you," he said. Serious.

"No, Ben, they didn't. If I knew you were in the hospital, I would have come."

"I asked them to call you. They said they called you and you never came."

"No one ever called me," I say, hoping I look worried. I hope I look pained at his news.

Ben is sad now. I think for a moment he might cry.

"Why were you in the hospital?" I ask gently.

"Malnutrition," he says easily.

I nod. I furrow my brow.

I have heard this story before. When we first started dating he told me his family took a week before visiting him in the hospital after he broke his leg as a ten-year-old.

"It's the only way I knew you would understand how alone I felt as a kid," he had said when he finally admitted he had never broken his leg. He had never been in the hospital as a child.

I wonder if Ben will keep pretending this has happened and, if he does, whether I should keep pretending to believe him. I wonder if Ben remembers telling the story about a childhood hospitalization when we first started dating.

I have heard this story before.

I keep looking at him, worried. Wondering. He keeps eating his half of the burrito. As he reaches for the Coke, his sad, serious face cracks into a smile and he laughs.

"You jerk!" I laugh, and smile.

I decide quickly to act like I am gullible and laugh at how easily I am fooled. "You shouldn't do that to people, especially people who believe you." I am joking and laughing as I say this.

Ben has a way of laughing where he scrunches his nose, closes his eyes, and nods his head up and down. It isn't really laughing, even though sometimes a guttural "huh, huh, huh" accompanies his scrunched face, like it does now. He's still laughing like this when I decide to keep eating.

He clears the trash from our meal, and I slide back into the red Fiat. Ben stays standing, looking at the Seven-Eleven we're parked in front of.

"I came here when things first started happening," he says, still looking at the store. "I was here for, I don't know, a toothbrush or something, and a girl from work was here and she didn't even recognize me."

He opens the Fiat door and gets in.

"Kate," he says, reaching for his seatbelt. "You know Kate."

"Yes," I smile to him. I know of Kate. A stranger to me, but not to him. Kate was a year ago.

"Anyway, I was in there, and I was looking so terrible she looked right at me and kept going, didn't know it was me."

I give him a face that I hope shows I'm interested and says "wow," without me having to say anything.

"What are we doing here?" he asks.

"Oh." I jump a little. "I was just listening."

"It's okay, you can listen and drive."

We decide to go home, and I'm behind the wheel. I like this, me driving. I never really did in our life together. It was easier to let Ben drive because I didn't care if he popped the clutch, or ground the gears, or used the wrong speed of the windshield wipers.

The sun is getting warmer as it rises in the sky, and I love this. Looking over at Ben, the California sun is turning his skin dark. He sits across from me, my handsome husband. I look down and smile to see his wedding ring shining in the sun. Our second wedding anniversary is in one month, and I already have a dress for the dinner we'll have to celebrate. I think of this dress, and think of that dinner, and I lean over to kiss his cheek. I'm nearly to his face when he pulls away, smiling.

"Hey!" I laugh. "I was so close!"

He laughs, too.

As we drive, he points out all the places where he's eaten recently. Down this busy street, he's eaten at nearly every restaurant.

"Hot dates?" I ask, smiling.

"Always with a group," he says quickly. "Big groups."

I smile. I believe him.

Somehow, money comes up. How it does, I'm not sure, because we're in a little red 1969 convertible with a grumble all its own. The noise of traffic is all around us, and the wind whisks words away before they reach ears. Somehow, here in this little convertible, driving down a busy road, money comes up. There is trouble here, and it is serious, and it is my fault.

"We can talk about it now," I say. "I don't care." I only have a little to hide, and there isn't much to tell to get to the truth. What I have to say can be said in spite of the Fiat's grumble, the wind, and traffic.

No, he shakes his head. "When we get home."

When we get back to the cottage, I don't know what to expect as I park the car, walk through the gate, and follow Ben past the French doors and into the main room.

He's full of energy, though. He might be happy, but I'm not sure anymore what it means when his eyes are dancing like they are now. He might be angry. I'm not sure.

"I can't believe you've wasted all that money," he says, sitting at the desk. I think he is laughing.

"I didn't waste it."

"Oh really?" His eyes are wide. "We need that money to get out of my lease and you said you had it."

"I do."

He's watching me.

"I did."

He's watching me.

"I will."

He looks away and shakes his head.

"No one would make you pay rent the whole year for an apartment you're not living in," I say defensively.

"You don't know that."

I did know, though. I also know enough to know it's not the landlord who will get my money if I give it to Ben.

"We can keep paying the rent on your apartment, and we'll find an apartment for us like the one today that we can afford on top of it. It will be okay. We'll be together."

"No," he says.

He's quiet, and I'm quiet.

I wait and look out the back door to watch Bugsy moving about. The day is still beautiful, and I wish we were back in the red convertible in the warm summer sun. I wish we were still in the world we were in an hour ago.

"This is what I'm going to do for you," Ben finally says. "Do you have paper?"

I get my sketchbook and flip to the back. Ben writes down all of our expenses, and then only his income because we will assume that I'll be in art school and not working. He shows me each number as he writes it down, every imaginable expense.

"And with my monthly income you subtract this and—"

The number Ben writes gives us plenty of money to keep paying rent at his apartment off the Five, in the canyon.

"See, it would work!"

"No," he says.

"There's plenty of money here, and you're not including my money from a student loan. It would work."

"It doesn't matter that it would work. It matters that you threw away all that money."

I don't even try to defend where the money went. It will only make Ben mad to hear he hasn't been paying bills, and that I was crying so much at work I couldn't work anymore, and that loans from my parents and grandparents have been my only income. The loans are the only way our lives have been paid for the last two months.

"You haven't changed a bit," he says.

I want to cry, but I want to figure out how to fix this more.

"It's not that much money. We can figure it out." I am begging.

"It's not the amount, it's that this is one more thing I'll have to fix. This is one more thing, and it might be the straw that breaks it all."

He's looking at me with tears in his eyes.

"I thought you had changed." The tears are full in his eyes. "But this takes everything away, everything. I just hope I can get over you. I'm just so afraid I won't get over you."

The tears are soon gone, and he stands. He moves to the middle of the room and he looks at me. Angry.

"You brought me here under false pretenses. You lied."

"No I didn't," I say. "This is so easy to fix."

"If I slept with someone else, I told you about it. If I did, then you knew. But you brought me here under false pretenses. You lied to me." He is staring, hard. "What else have you lied about?"

He waits for an answer, but I don't say anything. There is nothing.

"You haven't changed a bit."

"Ben, please," I say quietly.

"I'm going to have to think about this," he says, and stands there looking at me.

"Maybe I'll just lay down," he finally says.

He is smiling at me now as he passes by on the way to the bedroom. He's laughing a little and shaking his head. I'm not sure if he's still angry, or if somehow this will work out. We have enough money, after all, to pay for two apartments. I don't know what to do. Maybe it won't be an issue. I decide to wait. Not to say anything.

He closes the door to the bedroom, and I watch through a crack as he takes his sweater off to lie down.

"This won't work," he says, seeing me, putting the sweater back on.

"I'm sorry," I say and turn around.

He comes out, smiling. Really smiling. Eyes dancing. He radiates.

"I don't even know where to go," he says, pacing back and forth in front of me. He's bursting with energy.

I can feel it as he moves back and forth, back and forth in front of me.

"Don't go," I say. "Stay here and I'll go. You don't have to go anywhere." I jump up on the ottoman, looking down on him. "Or just stay here, stay with me." I smile. My eyes, I know, are pleading.

"No," he says. "I'll go to the beach for awhile."

"Okay," I say, still perched on the ottoman.

He comes close and holds me around the waist, his head just below my chin. I put my face in his hair, and look down at the tufts of familiar brown poking out from my fingers on the back of his head. I think for a moment he'll stay.

"I never left you, you know," he says. His voice is muffled a little, and sounds sad to me. "I never left you."

My heart aches and I hold my husband close to me and we stay here like this, melted together. He pulls away and asks if I'll be home when he gets back. I tell him I will be, I just have to take my aunt and uncle to the airport, but it won't take long.

"I guess the question is if you'll be here when I get back," I smile.

Ben shrugs. "We'll see," he says.

He comes back to me and holds me again, and I ask him one more time to please stay. He shakes his head no.

"This is just so—" I'm searching for the right word.

"Cruel?" Ben offers.

"Yes!" I say. "Yes." I say yes.

He pulls away again, and he's smiling. Really smiling. Toothpaste-commercial smiling.

I watch as he walks through the French doors.

I watch him drive down the driveway and wait for a break in traffic. I wave. He waves.

I watch as he drives away.

It is three in the afternoon. I have two hours before I take my aunt and uncle to the airport. I tell myself he won't be back before then. I tell myself to relax. I tell myself to go to the beach, or to take a nap. The nap sounds good.

I put on my cutest pair of pajamas, in case Ben comes home while I'm sleeping. The bed still isn't made, so I wiggle into the sheets and bury my face in the smell of Ben's pillow. I can't sleep, though. Every creak or groan from the cottage raises my head, hoping Ben will round the corner.

I lay here like this the whole afternoon. Waiting.

Finally, I leave for the airport and I know right away I've made a mistake. The traffic leaving the beach has slowed cars to a stop, and it takes me twenty minutes to go two blocks. I'm too late, and as I hang up the phone with my aunt, I know just how futile my wait for Ben has been.

The sun is falling below the trees on the other side of the street from the cottage, and I know that if Ben has spent the day on the beach he should be home soon.

Bugsy is ready for his evening walk, and we slowly go up and down the street in front of the cottage, waiting for a black Jeep to pass us. I duck into a quieter side street and call Ben.

"Wanted you to know I'll be eating in a little bit, and didn't want to assume you weren't coming home, so. Let me know if I should wait on dinner for you. Love ya."

We return to the main street. Bugsy is enjoying the slow pace and leaves no bush untouched. The cars passing us are starting to flash on their headlights, and I know I should go home.

I call my mother-in-law, who knows everything. She knows about the girl. Ben doesn't know his mother knows, and she and I work to keep it this way. She's been wonderful. She's answered every phone call. She tells me she loves me, and I know this is true. Talking to her is like being close to Ben somehow, and I need to hear her voice.

"Stay strong," she tells me when she hears that it seems Ben has disappeared again.

"I'm looking at a picture of you on your wedding day, and I just can't imagine you two not together," she says.

Neither can I. I can't imagine Ben not coming home tonight, but by now it's dark. Very dark. The lifeguard announcements have stopped. The traffic is slow.

"I love you," my mother-in-law says. "I'll be here."

I tell her I love her, too, and at this moment there is no one I can think of besides Ben whom I love more. She is the only one I have told the truth about the cottage to. She is the only one I have told the truth about the money to. She is Ben's mom, and right now she is my best friend. My confidante. If she knows the truth and still loves me, then there must be a chance for Ben and me.

We hang up, and I feel Ben's presence all around. The cottage is full of him, he's everywhere. I try his phone again, and it goes straight to voicemail. He's turned his phone off, which means he has seen my missed calls. He hasn't called back, and I know what this means, too. We've played this game before.

I wait to brush my teeth and go to bed, because I know when I do that I am giving in to the truth that I will do these things alone.

Tonight, I don't bother with the fan, or the curtain, or where Bugsy finds rest. I lay on my side of the bed

with the moon above me, full and bright in the window.
I can cry without worrying who will hear. I cry and ask
God what it is he wants from me. I roll onto my side
and look where Ben should be and try to picture him
there like he was this morning. Peaceful. Sleepy eyed.
My husband.

6

SATURDAY

It's before four in the morning, moonlight is shining in on me and my half-empty bed. Bugsy is having a dream in the main room. Other than Bugsy, the cottage is still with the night. I try not to think about where Ben might be. I think instead of what I will do when he comes home. What I will be wearing. What I will say. How I will smile.

I have been carrying a Bible with me for two months, and I ask it questions and open it randomly for an answer, as if it were a magic eight ball. I reach for my Bible on the bedside table and ask it to talk to me. By the light of the moon, it tells me what it always does: that it is more blessed to give than to receive. This makes me mad. I don't want to see this anymore. I want my bible to open to the story of the prodigal son who comes home, who is lost and then found and forgiven. It always opens to this, though. It always tells me that it is more blessed to give than to receive. I've had enough giving.

The dim first light of day begins to fill the cottage and I decide it would be better if I weren't here. Part of me wants to stay and wait for Ben, and the other part wants to run and never come back. But Bugsy is here and needs to be walked. The morning passes slowly. I call Ben twice, and his phone is still turned off. I fight the urge to cry and tell myself to be angry instead.

I know that what I have done with the money does not warrant this kind of response. Ben was so close, though, and if he could be that close after all we've been through, then another night of not knowing where he is sleeping isn't to be worried about.

I go out for a coffee, and find the book I wanted about surviving infidelity in a marriage at the bookstore. It's after noon now, and I think maybe Ben will be home.

Before I even pull into the driveway at the cottage, I see through breaks in the bushes that it is empty. I think maybe Ben has come and gone, but even as I think this, I know it isn't true. I call my friend Mandy from college and tell her Ben isn't home again.

"You tell him he can come home and be a husband, or he can take all his stuff and leave, that's what you do," she says. She is angry. "This isn't acceptable. He needs to be a man."

"I know."

"He needs to come home and from this night, or tomorrow night, or whatever, he needs to come home every night. Every night, he is home in bed with you. He is a husband. Period."

"He's not answering his phone, he has it turned off again," I tell her. Sad.

Mandy is quiet.

"This is craziness," she says.

We're both quiet.

"You shouldn't have to put up with this. Screw that, you shouldn't put up with this. This is your husband." She is angry.

I hang up the phone and take all of Ben's things, all of them, and pile them in the front room. I pack all of his toiletries, even the special bottle of shampoo. I sort through the laundry basket and stuff all of his dirty clothes in one of his suitcases. I move to the dresser to clear it of anything that's Ben's, and I see he has left his wedding ring. I also see his checkbook. I open it, and new checks for a new account that is all his lie crisply in line with one another. I flip to the back, and there they are, folded into each other. Two cashier's check stubs, each in the same amount. One is made out to Ben, and the other is made out to the girl. The total amount is big enough to be a security deposit on an apartment. I know the apartment is just off the Five, in a canyon. There is a deposit receipt to Ben's new account that shows where the cashier's checks went. I keep these things and hide them in the back of my underwear drawer. I'm glad I have packed Ben's things and piled them high for him to see as soon as he walks through the French doors.

With Ben packed, I have almost two hours before my motorcycle lesson. I have decided to do things that scare me, things that I might not otherwise do. Motorcycle lessons are the first on my list.

I write Ben a note that tells him I love him but that it was clear he was moving out again, so I made it easy for him by packing. I leave the note pinned to the front of the middle box.

It's hot out, and I decide to drive our blue Golf that is still hidden around the corner from the cottage. It will be nice to have air conditioning and be out of the sun for the drive to class. I haven't been able to listen to music, or watch television, or read since things started happening, but when I get into the car, I think that maybe I can. I flip through every station, but every song somehow reminds me that I don't know where my husband is. I drive to class in silence and call Ben once I get there. His phone is still off.

The class is small, full of couples. They've all come in nice cars, two by two, and some of them walk hand in hand. They offer each other snacks they've brought or the seat in the shade, and I try not to think about being here alone. I try to force myself to enjoy this new me. This new Jamie with a pierced nose, who could start art school on Tuesday, who is riding around a large, empty parking lot dotted with orange cones on a black motorcycle.

All I can think about is getting back to the cottage. I'm anxious to see if Ben has come home. I'm anxious to get there and have time to put everything back in case I've made a mistake in packing his things.

Sweaty and tired, I get into the car and am thankful for the cool air. I sit and call Ben, and this time I leave a message that tells him of what a good job I did in class. I tell him in the message that the instructor pointed me out as a good example. I tell him in the message I can't wait to go riding with him.

Ben isn't at the cottage when I get home, and he hasn't been there. But my brother has. He has left a note by the kitchen sink. My brother has seen all of Ben's things. My brother has probably read the nice note I left pinned to the front of the box in the middle.

My brother knows.

I hope he doesn't tell anyone else, even though I know he will, and I turn my phone off so I won't have to see when they start calling. So I won't have to hear their questions, their concerns. I know what their concerns are, but it's not their husband. It's not their marriage. I made a solemn vow to Ben and to God, for better or for worse. This is just our worse. I have taken a solemn vow. I have given my word.

I decide I can't sleep here tonight again alone, so I walk Bugsy before going to my aunt and uncle's.

"So we're back to leaving notes around the house," my aunt says as I come in the back door. "Your brother told us."

"Yeah," I say. I can't look at her.

"How did this come about?"

I don't want to talk about this, because my gamble to let Ben back in hasn't worked out. They live at the top of a hill so they have a wide view of the ocean, and I watch out the window while I wait for what I should say.

"Things aren't good," I finally say.

"Do you want to stay here?"

"Yes." I am grateful and hope I don't cry.

"What about the dog?"

"I walked him, and I'll go back in the morning to walk him."

"Okay," my aunt says, watching me closely. "Okay."

The back door opens and it's my brother.

"Hey," he says.

I wait for him to mention the cottage, but he doesn't. He is planning what to do tonight with my aunt. She goes upstairs to change, and we're left alone.

"So," he says.

"So you were at the cottage today," I begin.

"Yep," he says, dropping a handful of nuts in his mouth. He is chewing them and looking out the window.

The sun is slowly setting, and we watch as it slips behind the ocean.

"What was that all about?" my brother asks of the cottage. Of Ben's things.

"Ben's been to the cottage," I say.

"Uh, yeah," he says with another mouthful of nuts. "Want a beer?"

"No, thanks, still not there yet."

I haven't wanted to drink in months. I read alcohol enhances the mood you are in, and I don't care if this is true or not. I know I don't want the mood I'm in enhanced, and that's enough for me.

"This summer absolutely blows," my brother is

opening a beer. "We need to just go have some fun, get past this."

"Sorry," I say. "It's been hard."

"I'm sick and tired of really good girls wasting all of their time on complete losers."

"It's different. He's my husband. We're married."

"Whatever, it's not different."

"Marriage means something."

"Not when it's like this it doesn't."

"Well, it does to me."

My brother looks at me, hard.

"Where's your husband, Jamie? Let's go find him."

My heart sinks deeper into me.

"I don't know," I say quietly.

"Whatever. Tell Aunt Denise I'll be back."

I don't say anything as he leaves.

One of the cats who lives here comes over to say hello. I try to focus my attention on the cat and not think about where I might find my husband. My aunt comes downstairs and sees that my brother is gone. She knows not to ask where he is.

"He says to tell you he'll be back," I offer.

"Right," my aunt says. She is quiet. There is nothing here we want to say out loud.

I stay at home and let my aunt, uncle, and brother leave me and my sadness behind for the night. The Sea

World fireworks burst into the sky at ten, just as they do every night during the summer. I stop to watch them out of the back window until I think that if Ben is home in the canyon, then he is close enough to hear their crackling, too. I decide sleep will be a good escape, and I'm tired. So very tired.

I slide into the bed in the front bedroom that was mine while I didn't have a home and lie on my side to watch out the window. I've watched out this window since things first started happening, waiting to see Ben's black Jeep pull up outside. Waiting for Ben to get out, come to the door, to ask for me, to tell me he loves me. To tell me he can't believe he has done this to us.

Watching the street, I know he isn't coming. Finally, finally, I know I am here on my own. I know Ben is in an apartment he calls home. I know there is a girl who lives in this apartment who calls it home, too. I'm glad I have piled and packed all of Ben's things, and I think instead of leaving a love letter tacked to the box, I should go back and leave a note that tells him he's no man at all and I've wasted so much on him. But I don't. I lower the shade of the window so I can't watch the street anymore, roll to my side, and sleep.

7

SUNDAY

The deck is moist with dew, but I sit on it anyway. The backyard of my aunt and uncle's house is full of this deck, and it's perched so that the view is endless. I can see out over Ocean Beach, up to La Jolla where Ma and Papa live, over to Sea World.

Even now, as the sky moves from night to the first signs of morning, I can see the ocean glistening as it meets the land. Ben is only a few miles away, somewhere. I am here, tiptoeing around my aunt and uncle's house. I am here, trying to figure out what to do.

I have to walk Bugsy, so I decide to go to the cottage and get this over with. I feel bad for him there all alone, and I resolve to walk him all the way to Scripps Pier and let him play in the sand without being leashed.

The highway is clear, and I focus on the road ahead of me as I drive up the Five toward La Jolla Shores. I won't let myself picture Ben sleeping somewhere along this highway in a strange apartment, with a stranger.

It's still too early for beachgoers, so I get to the cottage easily and don't have to avoid parked cars along the street as I turn into the driveway.

Ben's black Jeep is here.

Ben is here.

It is Sunday morning, and I haven't seen Ben since Friday at three in the afternoon. He is here. He works today, and maybe he has come for a change of clothes. He is here.

Ben is here.

I walk through the French doors, and his things are still piled and packed as I left them. The note is still stuck to the front box. Ben rounds the corner, toothbrush hanging from his mouth, in a new bathing suit I've never seen.

"This is nice," he says, gesturing to his things. He is smiling.

"I couldn't bear to come home to an empty home again, so I did the packing for you." I'm watching him.

"I can't believe you did this," he's still smiling. His eyes are gleaming. He seems amused.

"You didn't call, you didn't answer the phone. I assumed you were moving out, so I helped."

He goes to the bathroom to spit toothpaste, runs water, and comes out rubbing his hands together.

"Thought you'd kick me out, did ya?"

He's still smiling.

"No," I smile and look down.

"You did!" He's joking.

"You didn't call or answer your phone. You just can't do that."

"We're not friends. We're not even friends, so why would I need to call you?"

"Ben."

"We're not even friends, that's how I can do that. You want to kick me out, you can kick me out. I told you that you would kick me out."

He's still smiling.

"Where did you go?"

"My apartment."

"Was your roommate glad to see you?"

"Yes. Both of them were."

"You never told me you had two roommates."

"You never asked."

I know his other roommate must be her daughter. Ben has told me her daughter is maybe three or four, and cute.

"Do you need to shower?"

"Already did."

"At your apartment?"

"Yep."

"Whose towels did you use?"

"I used what was there."

"Shampoo?"

"What was there."

Ben has been showering for months without his towel or shampoo, but for some reason today, right now, this bothers me.

"Those are nice shorts," I say of his bathing suit.

"Yeah, I had to buy them yesterday."

"Oh."

"I wanted to go to the beach, but all my stuff was here, so I had to buy these."

"I like them."

"Me, too."

"What did you do this weekend?"

"Went to the beach," he says, gesturing to his new shorts.

"That's it?"

"Yup, that's it."

I don't know what to say. I'm watching him, and he's smiling. I feel guilty for piling his things together.

"Do you want cereal?"

"Already ate."

"At your apartment?"

"Yep."

He digs through suitcases in the front room and then goes to the bedroom to get dressed. I stay where I am sitting. I don't know what to say. I don't know what to do. I just know I don't want to walk Bugsy right now, because Ben might not be here when we get back.

Ben comes out of the bedroom dressed for work and is sliding his wedding ring onto his finger. I feel guilty for packing his things.

"What will you do today?" he asks as he ties his shoes.

"Oh, lots to take care of."

"Job search?"

"Yep, job search for sure."

"Are you going to unpack my things?"

"I can," I say.

"No, no, don't. I want you to leave it all just as it is. Don't touch it."

"It's no trouble to unpack it."

"Leave it. I still can't believe you did that."

"I'm sorry."

He stands to go.

"Promise you won't unpack all this."

I look at him.

"Promise?"

"I won't touch it, Ben."

"Good. I'll see you tonight."

He comes close for a kiss goodbye and I follow him out the French doors to watch as he drives away, waving as he goes.

I take my time walking Bugsy. We stop at the bench where Ben said he thought he loved me and watch the waves roll in, one after the other. I ask God what he wants from me. I ask him what I'm supposed to do.

I don't know for sure, with absolute certainty, that Ben is living with this girl and that he was with her this weekend. I think maybe the cashier's checks are a mistake, or that they aren't for a deposit but something else entirely. I decide I should call his landlord and see if she can tell me about where Ben is living.

I have had her number for a week, and I have her name, things I have hidden away in my underwear drawer. I decide when I get back to the cottage that I will call her. I decide I will call her and then go see Ma and Papa, and our dog and cat.

She doesn't answer. But she hasn't answered every other time I have called, so I know to leave a message if I want to speak with her.

"Hi, my name is Jamie and I apologize in advance, this may be the strangest message you will receive. You rented an apartment about two weeks ago to my husband, his name is Ben, and I'm wondering if you could tell me a little about his living situation. I'm sure you can only imagine the circumstances under which a wife would be asking these things about her husband, and I'm just asking from one woman to another for a little information. I'm just trying to figure out what's going on. Thank you so much, and if you could keep this between you and me, I would greatly appreciate it."

I tell her how to contact me and I hang up. I'm happy with the message. I'm embarrassed, but I need information right now more than I need to maintain a good image.

I spend a little time with my grandparents, then the rest of the day I wait for her to call, and I look for jobs. I look for jobs in San Diego, and I look for jobs in Chicago, where my sister lives. Chicago, I have planned, will be my home if Ben chooses not to be married. I know I can't stay here in California. I know I will spend all of my time wondering where Ben is, looking for his Jeep. I call my sister and ask for help figuring out which neighborhoods would be good to live in. I take notes and add them to the printouts of jobs I have found.

I am still working on finding a job and waiting for Ben's landlord to call when I hear the rumble of Ben's Jeep in the driveway. He's home early, I think. Not even five. Then I think, he's home.

"Hey," he says, coming through the door.

"Hey." I smile. "How was your day?"

"Fine."

"Anything exciting happen?"

"Nope. You didn't unpack, did you?"

"I didn't touch a thing."

"Good."

"Do you want to go for a drive?"

"No."

"Walk to the beach?"

"No."

We decide to get dinner and drive down the road in the red Fiat. The sun is beating down, and as we get caught up in the crowds leaving the beach, I look over at Ben and am glad to see his face and his body moving beneath a shirt I bought for him last summer.

Dinner is like nothing has happened between us. Dinner is like he was here all weekend with me, driving in the Fiat, and going to the beach. We laugh, we finish each other's meals, we share a Coke and a cookie. We're here in a corner in the back of the restaurant, husband and wife. We're here laughing and talking, completing each other's sentences, and he puts his hand on my back to guide me through the tangle of tables in front of us when we leave. I love that to all the people in the restaurant we are a happily married couple. We are a young, happily married couple with their whole lives ahead of them.

"We should walk Bugsy," Ben suggests when we get back to the cottage.

I'm delighted at this suggestion. Ben seems to like Bugsy, and not even once has Bugsy hidden from Ben, or cowered when Ben comes close. This could be the dog to do what all the other animals couldn't.

My phone is flashing red with a call on the desk. It is our friend Russ from Kansas, and I know he is checking to see how I am doing because we haven't talked since before the holiday. I hide the phone while Ben gets Bugsy's leash so he won't ask what Russ and I have talked about.

Bugsy pulls us down the street until Ben stops at a lilac bush.

"Here," he says, plucking a flower from the bush, "do this."

He puts his lips to end of a small trumpet-shaped flower and sucks on it before handing me a flower to do the same. I put the end of the flower to my mouth like Ben did, and it's sweet on my lips.

"Wow," I say, surprised. "That's so sweet."

"Don't overexaggerate."

"Well, it's sweet."

"Not that sweet."

He walks away, annoyed.

"You're just like your mom," he says to Bugsy, not looking at me. "Everything is so fun, or so cute, or so wonderful, but it isn't. It's just sweet. It's not so sweet."

"I was expecting to taste something like a leaf, so to have something sweet was a surprise," I say, defending myself.

"Whatever."

He keeps walking.

Why did I have to say the word "so"? He's right, I think. Not everything is so incredibly anything. I wish I had just said "That's sweet!" and not said "so sweet." I catch up to him, and he points out a house he likes, and he talks about how our house will be different. We walk through the neighborhood, admiring these big, fancy homes, and I hold his arm. It doesn't matter anymore that he's been gone all weekend, or that I don't know where he woke up this morning. We have our wedding rings on.

A couple passes us, each holding tight to the hands of a small child in one hand. This cute little family on the way to the beach.

"Our kids will be even cuter than that," I say mischievously when they're out of earshot.

"What kids?"

"Our kids."

"We went into this deal agreeing that there would be no children."

I don't say anything. I don't mention Nigel, or Owen. I don't know what to say.

"Right?" he asks again.

I only know to smile.

We're quiet most of the way back, and Ben only yells at Bugsy once. This is incredible, I think, as I watch Ben talk to Bugsy in a Scooby-Doo voice. This is the dog who will do it.

We walk through the open French doors to the cottage and walk around Ben's pile of things to get to the main room.

"I just love that you did this," Ben says, smiling. "I still can't believe you did this."

I shrug. There is nothing safe here for me to say.

"I was really surprised to see all of this this morning," he says.

There is a moment here. I think to myself in this moment, really? Really, I think to myself. He's disappeared again, doesn't answer his phone, says we aren't friends, and there is surprise to find things packed? But the moment passes. I don't say anything.

"How about I beat you at chess?" he asks.

"Sure, you get the board, I'll get the pieces."

"What's this?"

Ben is holding up my notes on Chicago. I had left them on top of the board and hadn't thought of them again. With the notes is a timeline.

"'Move to Chicago, August first,'" Ben reads. "Wow, that's quite the plan you have here," he says, smiling. "Rogers Park. Good neighborhood, you might want to go further south though. Interesting."

He is looking at me and smiling.

"If you decide you don't want to be married I can't stay here," I explain.

"You should do what you want to do."

"I want to be with you."

"But you shouldn't be in San Diego just because that's where I am right now, you should go to Chicago if that's what you want to do."

"I only want to go to Chicago if you don't want to be married. I can't stay in this city and not be with you."

"That's ridiculous."

"We came here together, we planned for this together. I would want to enjoy all our hard work with you. Being here doesn't mean anything if it's just for me."

"You need to just pick a city and do it, and not based on what I'm doing."

"You're my husband."

"You just need to pick one and go for it."

I reach for the chess pieces.

"I'll do what's right."

Ben shakes his head, and shakes the papers in his hand. "This is interesting, though. Very interesting. It would be sad not to have you here."

He gets the board and we sit down to play, sorting pieces and carefully placing them on the board.

"You go first," he says. So I do.

"You're not even thinking about a strategy," he says a few moves later. "You need to focus."

I try to think only about the game and smile up at Ben now and then, glad to see him sitting across from me. He beats me easily, and we set the board for another game.

"Best two out of three," I say, propping my queen up in her square. "Loser buys winner candy of choice."

"Sure you want to make that kind of a bet?"

"Look out," I say, smiling.

Ben shakes his head, and is smiling, eyes shining. We both know he will win. Ben loves to win.

The next game goes as the first, even though I try my best to focus and anticipate Ben's moves. The third game, though, I go for Ben's pieces ruthlessly until he only has a handful left on the board.

"You aren't playing with strategy," Ben says. "You're just taking pieces without strategy."

"That's what the game's all about: taking pieces, taking names," I smile. I am winning.

"This is bullshit. You're just taking pieces without thinking."

"I'm thinking."

"No you aren't, you're just taking pieces."

We keep playing, and soon Ben has just his king and two pawns.

"This is bullshit," Ben says. "You cheated."

I know I haven't cheated, but I don't want trouble.

"I did take down a lot of your pieces," I offer. "I don't know why I took your rook, I could have done that differently."

Ben looks up at me and raises his eyebrows. His hands are folded at his chin, and he's angry. The game is over.

"Let's go," he says.

"Candy," I smile.

We get in the red Fiat, Ben is driving. We drive down the main drag of La Jolla Shores to the gas station just at the edge. Pulling in under one of the lights, someone walking by asks what year the car is.

"Sixty-nine," Ben smiles. He is proud of it. "It's in great condition, too."

"Looks like it," the stranger smiles back and keeps walking.

We have fun dancing around each other in the store. The lights are bright, and it's a shock of the real world coming from our little cottage. We're here together, and I love looking over the aisles seeing Ben smile at me. We've done this a million times, too. We did this across the country last summer, with our dog and our cat waiting in the rental truck packed full of our wedding gifts and furniture.

I'm glad for a moment that we don't have any of this anymore. I'm glad for the garage sale last month where pickup trucks with Baja California plates lined up at six in the morning in front of our Park Boulevard apartment, filled with people who had come to take from our home the things we had used to define our lives together. I'm glad that we can just go back to this rented cottage filled with someone else's things and just be us.

We drive home slowly, past the beach, looking up at the night sky. This is exactly what we talked about when we talked about coming to California. We did it. We're here. Together.

We talk in British accents, bad ones, just for fun. I tell him I can't wait to take him to London, to show him where I lived, and all my favorite places.

"We'll go someday, love," I say with an accent.

"I can't wait," he says, and sounds more Australian than British.

After our candy, and after we put the chessboard away, we dance around each other again at the sink. I have brought my electric toothbrush specifically because of Ben, because he hates when I don't use it. I don't want to make him angry by using my plain toothbrush, so as we move around each other, the buzz of my electric toothbrush fills the air.

I close the curtains in the bedroom, so the moon doesn't shine in on Ben, I turn the fan on its side, I send Bugsy out to the backyard to rest, I put my phone in a drawer in case anyone calls. By the time Ben comes to bed, I'm ready.

His face is illuminated by the glow of the bedside lamp, and he looks sweet to me. He looks like my husband. I watch as he takes his wedding ring off and places it on the dresser, then his glasses. I see he has placed his ring on top of mine, and I love that our two rings will spend the night together like they have a million times, mine fitting perfectly in the circle of his.

Everything is perfect. The fan isn't humming, the moon isn't shining, and Ben crawls into bed beside me, turning off the lamp. I lay there, waiting to see what he does, and soon, he rolls over and faces me.

"I love you, Ben," I say watching him.

"I love you, too."

I can see his eyes glistening in the darkness, just

inches from my face, and I melt into the bed and lose myself in the thought that this will somehow work. I got everything right tonight. Ben is back beside me, his foot has reached for mine under the sheets and we lie here like this, his foot warming mine, his face just inches from mine, as we drift off to sleep.

8

MONDAY

When I hear the shower start, I don't get Bugsy. Instead, I run to Ben's Jeep and look for his cell phones. He has two: one for work, and the one we got in Kansas. I turn them on, impatient. I can't hear from here in the driveway if the shower is still running, and I don't want to get caught. Hurry, I think, watching as the phones turn on. Hurry.

I'm shaking as I press the buttons. Call history. Outgoing calls. Incoming calls. Missed calls. I go through them all. He called her twice this weekend, just five minutes apart on Saturday. He has called another coworker, Frankie, nine or ten times. Maybe he stayed with Frankie this weekend, I think. He only called her twice, I think. She only called him once. Frankie only called him once. Maybe he stayed with Frankie. There is a new number for her. He has it listed as her home number, and all I have is her cell phone. I put the phone down and run to the cottage. I'm shaking hard, my heart pounding as I quietly dig for a pen and paper. The shower is still running. Racing back to the Jeep, I take down the new number on a yellow Post-it Note, the numbers squiggly from my shaking hand. I have done this before. This is how I got his landlord's number a week ago.

I turn off the phones and put them back exactly as I found them. I run to the other side of the Jeep, looking up at the open French doors of the cottage, hoping I don't see Ben standing there, but all I see are his boxes of things, with my note to him still pinned to the front.

The glove compartment has the tags and receipt from his bathing suit. He must have changed in the Jeep, I think. Maybe he really did stay with Frankie. Maybe he didn't see her this weekend after all. Maybe he is living with Frankie, and not her.

There is nothing left to search, and I run back to the cottage, careful not to let the gate make any noise as I go through it. The shower is still running and I whisper for Bugsy, who has come into the cottage while I investigated Ben's car.

"Let's walk," I whisper, gesturing frantically. "Come on."

I grab his leash and wave it and he comes running.

We run quietly through the gate, down the driveway, and stop when we get to the main road. Ben won't suspect anything, I know. He'll just think we've been walking. I feel in my pocket for the yellow Post-it with her home phone number, and am glad it's there and didn't fall to the cottage floor in my haste.

A block away, Bugsy and I slow down. I have at least ten minutes before Ben is dressed for the day, so Bugsy and I walk to the beach. I need to calm down. I need to relax. All I've done is look at his cell phones, look at bathing suit tags, and taken down a phone number. But I feel like maybe if he knows I have done these things that it will be unforgivable.

Bugsy and I walk the boardwalk up the beach, and we're whistled at by a group of surfers making their way to the water. I smile. Ben has told me I'm too thin, that I don't look good, and I'm glad that someone, even if it is a stranger in this crowd of faces, thinks to whistle at me as we walk by. I'm in green shorts and a tank top, hair pulled into a lopsided ponytail, and I'm whistled at. This is good, I think. Maybe Ben isn't right.

Ben is still here when we get back, and I look carefully in his Jeep as Bugsy and I pass. Everything looks like Ben left it. Ben shouldn't suspect I've searched every corner.

I can hear from the gate that he is playing a CD

I bought for him, listening to the song I told him I thought he would like. I love that he is playing it. It's always been my job to introduce Ben to new things, and this morning I am again with this music. Ben is in the Hawaiian shirt I bought for him at Old Navy, and he asks if he looks okay.

"I love it," I say.

"Do you think it's too much for work?"

"I think it's perfect."

"You would say that. What do you really think?"

"I really think I like it. You look good."

"Whatever. I'm fat."

"You're not fat." I'm sick of hearing this. He isn't fat. His pants are falling off of him, his smallest belt on the very last hole.

"I'm going to mass in about an hour. Any special requests?" I ask.

"Nope."

"I've got a straight line to the big JC, so anything you can think of, I'll talk to him about." I'm smiling.

Ben shakes his head.

"Will you call today about our laptop?" he asks.

"Sure, anything else?"

"Did you call about our deposit?"

"Yes, it's on the way to our P.O. box."

"Will you check for it today?"

"Yes."

"Are you going to look for a job?"

"Yup."

"You know you'll have to take that out when you start interviewing," he points to my nose ring.

"I know, but it's fun for now."

He goes to the desk to write down what he wants me to do today and sees a card I have written his mother.

"This is interesting," he says.

I have written her a thank you, and at the end I have written, "I will keep trying to do what you say—to let go, and let God."

"What is this?" he asks, pointing to this last line.

"Your mom tells me this a lot. She's been wonderful."

Ben says nothing, is thoughtful.

"We just talk girl talk," I tell him. "Don't worry, it's just all girlie stuff."

He doesn't care. He goes to the bathroom for lotion, and I go to the bedroom, just to move and look like I'm busy and not just waiting for him to leave. I see his wedding ring, still encircling mine, and I pick it up and roll it around my pointer finger.

"Here you go," I say, holding it out to him when he comes into the main room.

"Oh, thanks," he smiles.

He fits the ring over his finger and kisses me good-bye. I walk him through the French doors past the pile of his things, and as I hug him in the warm morning sunlight, he tells me again not to unpack for him.

"I won't touch it, geesh," I smile. "Have a good day."

"You, too," he smiles, and I watch him wave as he drives away.

I decide not to go to church. I can't sit still long enough, and I don't understand the priest, and I don't want to dress up so I fit in with the crowd in this fancy neighborhood. I go instead to my grandparents', to Ma and Papa to see Huey and my cat, Captain Jack. I take our blue Volkswagen from around the corner. Maybe I will wash it today while I'm out. On the way to Ma and Papa's, I stop for coffee for Ma and me, and my phone rings as I balance the cups to get into the car.

It's Ben's landlord from the apartment off the Five, in the canyon.

"Hello?"

I hope I don't drop the coffee. I hope I don't sound as nervous as I am. I hope I don't sound desperate.

"Hi. I'm just returning your message," she says. She sounds nice. I don't want to put her in the middle of things, but I want to know about this apartment off the Five, in a canyon.

"I know you can't tell me much, but I'm wonder-

ing if you can just tell me if he is living with a woman,"
I say. Trying to make this sound like a normal request.
Like I'm asking her if she has any available units or
how much a deposit will be.

She pauses. I know she is considering how much
she can tell me and still be professional, still maintain
certain parameters.

"Yes," she finally says, "he is."

I'm quiet.

"This must be very difficult for you," she offers.

"He moved out suddenly, and left me to take care of
our apartment, and all of our things, and left me without a home," I say, and I don't know why I'm telling her
these things.

"Can you tell me if a little girl also lives there?"

"I'm sorry, I really can't."

I say the girl's name, and ask if she can tell me if
this is my husband's roommate.

"I'm sorry, I can't tell you that," she says, and I can
tell by her voice she really is sorry. "But I can tell you to
trust your gut."

"Thank you," I tell her. "Thank you."

"You sound like a really nice person and you
deserve better than this," she says. "You deserve a good
man, not someone who would do this to you."

I know she is right. I want to ask her how Ben and

the girl presented themselves. As roommates? As boy-friend and girlfriend? As husband and wife? But I don't.

"Is there more than one bedroom?" I ask instead. Maybe they are just roommates.

"Well, it's a townhouse, so yes, there is more than one bedroom." I can tell by her voice that she feels sorry for me, asking if there is more than one bedroom. I can tell by her voice that she knows what I know, that it doesn't matter if there are five bedrooms or one.

"Take care of yourself," she tells me. "You'll be okay."

I hang up the phone and look at the coffees now sit-ting in the cup holders of the car Ben and I pretended our children were buckled into the backseat of. The car we brought all the way from Kansas a year ago. The car I plan to wash today so Ben won't see the splashes of brown dirt along the side.

He probably didn't call her this weekend because he was with her, I think. I know this is true. I've known it all along, but I don't know how to work the story in my head any more so that there are other possibilities.

He wore his wedding ring today, I think. He kissed me goodbye and told me to have a good day. He is com-ing home to me tonight. He has to.

I go to Ma and Papa's, and Huey greets me at the

back gate. Ben still hasn't asked about Huey, or Captain Jack. He hasn't asked where they are or what they are doing. I haven't brought them up because I don't want to bring up unpleasant things with Ben until things are more stable. So I haven't told him they are here and doing really well.

"I talked to his landlord," I tell Papa.

My grandfather shakes his head and invites me to the backyard to sit.

"His roommate is a woman."

"You've known this, Jamie," Papa is frustrated. I can feel his disbelief. "You've known this how long?"

"Well, I didn't really, really know until just now," I say.

"Come on, Jamie. We've been over this."

"I know."

The coffee is hot and burns my tongue. I don't care, and take another sip. It burns my tongue again and then my throat as it goes down.

"What are you going to do?" Papa asks.

I don't know, so I don't say anything.

"Now this girl," Ma starts, "do you know her?"

I shake my head, no.

"Are you sure he's living with her."

I nod my head, yes.

"And her little girl?"

I nod my head, yes.

There are no words between the three of us. We watch as Huey digs a hole in the corner under the orange tree, dust billowing around where the deck used to be.

"What are you going to do?" Papa asks again.

I still don't know, so I don't say anything. I'm not sure what I can do. I need a job. I need a home. I need to rewind two months and stop this before it starts.

They walk me out the front door and tell me they love me. I look out at their view, just blocks from the ocean, and the day is spectacular. It hasn't started to heat up, and the sun is still gentle as it shines down on their white house here in La Jolla. I wave goodbye as they sit with Huey in front of the house and wave until I turn the corner to head toward the coast.

Parking my car underneath the trees a few blocks down I ask my Bible a question before getting out to go down to the water. Down the stairs, turning once, twice, to the huge rocks below. I sit there and watch the waves come in. I ask for awareness. I ask for truth. I ask for strength. I ask God to help Ben. I ask God to please, please help me.

A big wave comes crashing against the rocks and

reaches up for me, wetting my feet. I sit here like this until I'm uncomfortable from the sun, and the hard rock that's my seat, and I decide to go to my aunt and uncle's. Maybe they will be able to tell me what to do.

"What's the latest?" they ask as I come through the backdoor.

"He's living with her," I say.

"Oh come on, you knew this."

"I know, but now I know it. I called his landlord."

"Lord."

"I know. Pathetic."

"Not pathetic, just—you knew already, right?"

"Yeah, but I had to know for sure. Now I do."

"Did they tell you he was living with her?"

"No, she just said he was living with a woman."

Everyone is quiet for a moment.

"I think Ben is sick," I say.

"Seriously," my aunt agrees.

My uncle throws the dishtowel in his hands on the counter. "Nah," he says. "He's not sick. I see this every day down at the beach."

"Oh but come on, this is a little extreme, don't you think?" my aunt asks.

"Well, maybe, but is this really all that unique of a situation?"

"Lonnie." My aunt has her chin down, eyes up.

"I don't know," he says. He looks like he's holding his breath. Like he's holding words in his mouth. "It's tough."

"What's next?" my aunt asks me.

I shrug. I don't know.

They've had enough of this. They're all ready to see me move to the next thing. I haven't been able to. I can't imagine this has happened. I can't imagine Ben is gone.

He's not gone, though, I think. He's at work. He's just at work. I decide to call him when my aunt and uncle go upstairs.

I go out to the deck that looks out over San Diego, and I call Ben. He answers. I talk in a British accent, but he has no time for it so I try to talk business.

"I called the laptop people," I say. "It will be a few weeks for them to fix it."

This annoys him. He is angry by this. I shouldn't have called.

"That's all I have, really I just wanted to hear your voice," I tell him. I am pretending nothing is wrong.

"Hmm," he says.

"I love you dearly." I am pretending it is two months ago.

"Hmm."

And we hang up.

I never get to washing the car, but I do check the P.O. box for our deposit check, which isn't there. I spend the rest of the day trying not to think about what I now know and get the cottage ready for Ben to come home. He is coming home.

Everything is ready, and when he walks through the door, setting his keys on the boxes in the front room, the cottage looks perfect. The pillows on the bed are balancing on their corners—sideways, like diamonds. The rug is straight. The dishes are clean. It sparkles.

"I'm going to the beach," he says.

"Fun! Can I come?"

"I don't care what you do."

"Good, then I'm coming."

We change and walk to the beach with one towel between us.

"How was your day?" I ask as we walk side by side down the sidewalk.

"Fine."

He is quiet. He doesn't want to talk. I don't know what I can say.

When we get to the beach the warm summer air is just perfect for a swim in the ocean. Laughter and screams of happiness pop up from the crowd sprawled on the sand in front of us.

"Can you believe we live here?" I ask. "This is just too beautiful."

Ben doesn't say anything. He drops the towel, kicks off his flip-flops, and takes off his shirt.

"I'm going in," he says.

I follow him. We wade out into the water until it's up to our chests and we smile at each other, waiting for a wave. Ben dives under the water and shoots up, wiping his eyes clear, smoothing his hair back.

The water feels good. It's warm, and the waves are gentle as they swell past us. I swim over to Ben, and slide my arms underneath his, and hold his wet body close. He puts his arms around me, and we stay like this until a wave comes that is strong enough to break us apart.

"You're cold. You should go in," he says.

"I'm okay."

I stay and try to ride a few of the bigger waves as long as they will carry me, and I can't help but laugh every time I reach the surface after one pulls me under water, leaving me without air. I'm in the ocean with my husband, laughing as the waves crash down around me, and he laughs back. It is as it has been from the beginning of us: him and me against the world. I watch as he rides a wave as far as it will take him, and I'm glad I was able to give him this. This boy from Kansas who wanted to get as far away from home as he could, and I helped him. I brought him here to the edge of the country, to the warm summer waters of the Pacific. We are such a long way from home.

We slowly make our way to the shore, and I let Ben towel off first. I wait for him to take the towel and wrap me up in it like he used to, but instead he throws it at me when he's finished. That's okay, I think, and dry myself off. I have lost a silver hoop earring in the sand, but I don't want to make a big deal of it. I want to keep moving, keep this night moving toward good. I haven't said anything wrong yet, and I know that instead of being at his townhouse with his new roommate he is here with me. There still might be hope here.

"I love that we can do this," I say as we walk down the boardwalk.

"It's pretty cool."

"I'm still glad I married you," I say.

He's quiet.

"I know, I know, you're probably leaving me tomorrow, but I don't care. I still love you."

"That's not a very good attitude."

"It's true, though, isn't it?" I say. I'm smiling. He isn't.

"It's not a very good attitude."

He watches the sidewalk in front of him, and we turn to begin our walk home.

"So another thing I've been wondering," I ask as we walk.

"What's that?"

"About finding forgiveness." I stop. I wait.

Ben says nothing.

"My faith says that it's not a human virtue, that it takes God to help us forgive. So what do you think?"

"I think you just forgive."

"So you say the words 'I forgive' and it's done?"

"Yes."

"That's all there is to it?"

"Yes."

I don't believe this. I don't believe him.

We leave wet footprints from the beach to the cottage and take turns showering the salt water off of us. The beach towel is hung to dry, Bugsy is walked, and we sit down at the desk to figure out what comes next.

Ben is looking up Jeep engines on the Internet.

"Wouldn't you just rather have a 1969 red Fiat than a new engine?" I joke.

"I already have one of those," he shrugs, and keeps looking.

We look at what motorcycles we will buy now that I

know how to ride, and as he pulls up a small Kawasaki to investigate his phone buzzes with a message. It is a text message from her, she is asking him to call. It is an emergency.

"She never calls this phone anymore," he says.

He sits for a while before getting up.

"I'll be right back," he says, taking his phone and leaving the cottage.

I want to tell him no, don't call her. I want to tell him he is here with his wife, he shouldn't dare call her. She shouldn't have dared call him.

I want even more for him to come back, though. For him to stay. I don't say anything and watch as he walks away.

I want to follow him, to hear what he is saying, but there is nowhere outside that will hide me well enough. I have to just let him go. I watch as he walks away.

I decide to do his laundry while I wait. A half hour passes before my phone rings.

"Are you hungry?" he asks.

"Starving."

"Good, let's go get dinner. I'm sorry I took so long."

"That's okay," I say even though it's not okay. It's so far from being okay, but I don't know what to say.

"I'm just around the corner, but I'm walking fast, so grab some keys."

I take the Fiat keys, and as I leave the French doors of the cottage, Ben turns the corner.

"I'm so nervous right now," he says as we meet at the Fiat. "Get in and I'll tell you about it."

We sit, and the sun has gone down, so I watch Ben and wait in the darkness.

"That was her," he says. "But you knew that."

I don't say anything.

"She never calls that phone anymore, so." He doesn't finish.

I don't say anything.

"She called, and I tried to be nice and everything, told her we missed her at softball on Thursday night, but she was really mad. I guess someone at work is going to be fired, and she thought I knew something about it or maybe that it was me who was getting fired. I kept telling her I didn't know, why would I know, but she insisted I did."

I don't say anything. I know this is all a lie. But I don't stop him.

"What are we doing here?" he asks.

"I'm just listening," I say.

"That's okay, listen and drive, I'm hungry."

So I start the little Fiat, turn on the headlights, and pull out onto the main street.

"Real quick, where do you want to go?"

"Wherever, you pick."

"So?" I ask.

"So, I told her I didn't know anything, and that's pretty much it."

The first restaurant we try is closed.

"Sorry," Ben says. It is his fault we are eating so late.

The next restaurant is closed, too. We can eat in their bar, but we don't want to. As we come out of the second restaurant to get back into the Fiat, Ben is shaking his head, smiling.

"What?" I ask.

"I was pretty mean to her," he says. "You know how I can get."

"Oh, I know," I say. And I do.

"She hung up on me." He is smiling. I have hung up on him before. In the beginning.

"Maybe we got disconnected." He thinks for a moment, then, "No, she hung up on me. I feel bad."

"Oh well," I say. "How about Taco Bell?"

"Sure."

We drive through and find a spot along the seawall to sit and eat our tacos. The moon is shining bright on the ocean to our left, and we eat in silence. We're hungry. We pass the Coke back and forth between us until we are sucking at the bottom.

"Ready?" he asks.

"I want to see what's on the other side of the wall, then I'll be ready."

I jump out to run across the street. I've been wondering the whole meal if it is a cliff or a beach, if the water is right up against the wall or if it is a hundred yards away.

It is a steep cliff, a drop of two stories from the wall to the rocks below. I wouldn't have thought this from where we sat in the Fiat across the street. It looked much more innocent than this big drop. I look back at Ben to tell him, and he's watching me. He's too far to yell, so I turn back to the ocean.

Turning my head up to the sky, stars are shining bright in the blackness. I open my arms wide. Thank you, God, I think. Thank you for this moment. I turn back to Ben and smile as I jog around the front of the Fiat. He smiles back, and before long we're winding our way up the coast home. We drive through downtown La Jolla, cruising, letting the wind come between us, swirling and dancing until we come to a stop sign, when the world becomes still for a moment. We stop and start like this until we pull into the cottage, turn off the rumble of the car, and are left with the quiet of home.

"Up for a game?" he asks.

"Sure."

"No bets tonight, just play."

"Sure."

He beats me easily the first game. As we set up the board for the second, I watch as he smiles to himself, placing pawns in their squares.

In less than a dozen moves, I have him in checkmate. He didn't see me coming, and I can't believe he's missed it. I don't care if he's angry.

"That was lucky," he says.

"That was strategy."

"Whatever. It was luck."

"I know what I'm doing."

"Whatever."

We're done with games. It's time for bed. We have a routine now, and I wait for him to settle in beside me. When he does, he turns his back to me, and I wonder if I should turn over and hold him. I wait for a moment, then I do.

The cottage is still, and everything is behaving as it should. We lay in the quiet of our home, and my eyes are slowly begging for rest. I am here with my husband. I am here at home with my husband. The world is as it should be.

"I think I'm your crutch," he says to the darkness.

I don't say anything. This doesn't make sense to me.

"I'm your crutch," he says again.

I hold him and am quiet. My head is on his pillow. We're close. I watch my arm go up and down with
his breathing. I can smell his hair, I am trying not to
breathe on his neck.

"Good night," I whisper. "I love you."

The darkness is still. The darkness is all around.

9

TUESDAY

"Why are you up?" He's angry. Really angry.

Ben is up early, very early, so I am up, too, returning from Bugsy's walk.

"Thought I'd start my day," I say with a smile.

"You'll notice I packed everything." He is steady.

"Oh?"

"I packed everything in case I decide today to leave you."

"Oh?"

"I should probably take everything now to save the driving, but, oh well."

I sit down on the chair in the main room.

"I'm your crutch," he says, sitting at the desk to put his shoes on. "You can't be the person you're supposed to be with me around."

I don't know what this means. I don't care. I know what is happening.

"So you'll move back into the townhouse with her, then?"

He stops and stares at me, hard.

"So you'll move back into the townhouse, then?" I ask again.

"I'm not living with her." He is adamant. "And it's an apartment."

"I know you're living with a woman in a townhouse."

He is angry. He is about to rage. He starts to say something but walks out the open French doors instead. I run to the bedroom and grab the wedding ring I know is still sitting there and chase him outside to his Jeep.

"Marry me?" I ask, holding it up to him as he pulls his seatbelt on.

"No," he says, taking it from me and putting it on his left ring finger anyway. "Here, I'll wear it on this hand," he says, moving it to the right. "That's a hell no."

I stand and wave as he pulls away. He doesn't look back. I know he is gone. It is early. Very, very early, and I know when he leaves me that he isn't going to the office. I know he will make a stop at the townhouse just off the Five, in a canyon, where she lives. Where I know he will live again, too.

I could have started art school today, but I never finished my sketches. Never filled out forms for financial aid. So instead of art school, I look for jobs in Chicago. I write cover letters, print résumés. I get a call for an interview down the street. I have applied for a job at a surf shop a few blocks away, back when I thought I'd be here, back when I thought I could be a Southern California surfer wife. I agree to be there in an hour, and I rush to get ready.

In the shower my nose ring falls out, and I can't find it on the tile floor. It's gone. It has probably washed down the drain, and I give up looking for it.

Wearing a cute skirt and tank top, I walk to my interview and hope that it will be over in time for me to be home when Ben gets there.

"You're really educated and had a great career. Why do you want to work in a surf shop?"

This is the first question. We're in the backroom, with T-shirts and surfboards piled high all around. I'm meeting with the store owner, and I can tell she's curious to know my answer. I know the only thing that will really answer the question is the truth.

"My husband just left me for another woman, and I need something different," I say. This is the truth.

"Wow, I'm really sorry," she says.

She has a wedding ring on, and I know she really is sorry. I have my wedding ring on, too, and I know right now it doesn't mean what hers does.

The interview goes well, really well. I'm glad I can do this so well under the circumstances. I need a job. Ben will be impressed if I get a job. I can pay my father and grandfather back if I get a job. I walk home satisfied, and stop at the grocery store on the way to pick up fresh flowers for the table at the cottage, and Ben's favorite snack.

I hear him pull up the driveway, but I don't go out to meet him. I stay at the desk, pretending to diligently work on job applications. I hear him behind me as he walks through the door.

"Hey," he says.

"Hey, how was your day?"

"Fine."

He sees the snacks I got for him, and takes them to the chair across from me. I turn my chair around to face him and watch him eat. I tell him about my interview. He is glad it went well and listens as I tell about the surfboards piled high and all around in the backroom. He laughs.

"I asked around at work today and no one knew what she was talking about last night. No one is going to get fired," he says when I finish.

I can't believe he's continuing this story. I know she didn't call to talk about work last night, but I let him tell his lies anyway. And he does, he talks about work, about where he went today, who he saw. About who would get fired if someone were going to be, about how if anyone really looked at his work that he would be fired easily.

"Every day I worry someone will look close enough at my records to know I'm not doing my job," he says.

"You'll be okay." I am encouraging.

He is quiet.

"I was really pissed off this morning," he says.

"I know."

I am quiet.

"How did you know it's a townhouse?" he asks.

"When I was a little girl, I loved Nancy Drew. Do you know Nancy Drew?"

He shakes his head, no. I am trying to buy time while I figure out how much I want him to know.

"Well, I loved her. I wanted to be her. She solved mysteries that no one else could. *Harriet the Spy*, too. Did you ever read that?"

He shakes his head, no. He is still waiting for an answer.

"It wasn't hard to find out. I just did a little sleuthing."

"What does that mean?"

I know he doesn't know what sleuthing means, but I don't care to tell him.

"You tell more than you need to when you lie, Ben. I know you well enough to know. You've told me more than you would want to."

He keeps eating his snack and is thoughtful. He is here. My husband is home, eating his favorite snack. He has actually told me about his day, and told me about his work. Maybe we will go for dinner when this is done. He rolls up the bag and stands.

"Well, I guess that's it," he says. He puts the snacks away, and I watch from my chair as he goes to the front room and picks up a box.

"What are you doing?" I am at his side and asking, even though I know exactly what he's doing.

"Moving out," he says simply, taking the box to his Jeep.

"Ben, please," I beg.

He is angry.

"Did you follow her home from work? Is that how you know? Did you? Did you sit and wait for her to come out and follow her home?"

"I don't know what she looks like, or what kind of car she drives."

"Leave the poor girl alone, Jamie, just leave her alone."

He has another box and pushes past me out the French doors.

"Please don't do this. Please don't leave me." I am pleading.

"I left you a long time ago."

"You didn't even try! Do you think troubles won't happen with her? Do you think the same things won't happen with her? They will! They just will."

"Is that a threat?"

"No! It's the truth! So stay here with me and figure this out, I'm your wife."

"No."

"But I know you like no one else does. I know your dark sides and I love you anyway. I know your history. I know where you've come from. I love that we've known each other since we were teenagers. Please, Ben."

"What if I just go back to Kansas and find your friend Mandy, I bet she'd marry me. She's known me even longer than you have."

I am quiet. I don't know what to say.

"You can go find your beautiful Brian, you've known him as long as you've known me. Go find him."

I am quiet. I don't know what to say.

"I've changed so much, I've fixed everything I could, and just with what I've done we'll be so much better."

He stops. "You haven't changed at all."

"How can you say that?" I'm beside myself. "The nose ring," I start.

"You took it out."

"It fell out in the shower this morning."

"Sure it did."

"And I had an interview, you even said I would have to take it out for an interview. What about the motorcycle lessons. Art school. Surfing. Living in a cottage by the ocean." I am counting these things out on my fingers. "I chose this cottage, I chose this home. I invited you into my life."

"I chose this a year ago," he says.

"My home will always be open to you, but—"

"Here it comes, but what? It's okay, here comes the rage, let it out. You hate me."

"I don't hate you."

"It's okay, get angry, come on."

"My home will always be open to you, but next time—"

"Next time what?"

"Next time, if you're certain—"

He puts down his box and turns to me with tears in his eyes. "I don't know if I'll ever be certain again."

I don't know if he's talking about me, or about anyone, or about anything. He is about to cry.

"Please be certain next time," I ask of him again.

"So, I can come back to more lies? You lied to get me here. I come back again and what lies will you have told?"

"You know everything," I say quietly. "Everything. There are no lies."

"And I'm supposed to believe that?"

He keeps packing his Jeep. Back and forth, back and forth, between the cottage and this black Jeep with Kansas plates that I bought for him.

The room is slowly emptying, and he comes in for a pile by the door. I grab his arm. I am inches from his face. He is angry, his almost-tears are long gone.

"So this is it?" I ask.

"Do you want a divorce?" I ask.

He shrugs. "Do what you need to do," he says.

"This is a big deal, though, Ben. This is a marriage. Things will have to be handled. There are things we should talk about."

"It's not that big of a deal, do what you need to do," he says again, and moves to bring the guitar I bought for him to the Jeep. He turns in the driveway, sun shining in his eyes. "You gave me this," holding it up, "do you want it back?"

"Yes," I say, hard.

He laughs and shakes his head and turns to bring it to the Jeep anyway.

"You know," he says, coming back into the cottage, "this whole time I was here I was trying to figure out if I was here because I wanted to be or because of my guilty conscience. I think I just wanted to see that you were going to be okay."

"I am not going to be okay." There are tears in my eyes. I let them fall. "I am not going to be okay."

We are quiet.

"So you don't love me anymore?" I ask.

He is quiet.

"Do you love her?"

"Would it make it easier for you if I said I did?"

"Nothing would make this easier."

"Would it make it easier if I told you she's pregnant and we're getting married on a cliff overlooking the ocean?"

"Nothing would make this easier."

There are only two boxes left before Ben is gone. I stand watching through the French doors as he takes one, leaving one last box in the middle of the cottage.

"If you leave, how am I supposed to forgive myself?" I ask him. The tears are wet on my cheeks when he comes back for the last box.

"Forgive yourself?" he asks.

"I can deal with everything you've done, but how am I supposed to forgive myself?"

He shakes his head. He doesn't have an answer. He doesn't understand why I've asked this, and neither do I.

He walks past me with his last box, out the French doors. Bugsy is there.

"Bye, Bugsy, bye, bye," he says in his Scooby-Doo voice, "nice knowin' ya." He walks through the gate, letting it slam behind him. When he gets to his black Jeep, he lifts the last box in with the rest. Putting a hand on the door, he looks back at me.

"Talk to you later." He smiles, with a small wave. He seems happy.

I watch as he gets in the Jeep, piled high once again with everything he claims as his own. I watch as he drives down the long driveway, leaving the red Fiat, leaving Bugsy, leaving the cottage. Leaving me. He doesn't look back. He doesn't turn around to see me in the driveway, in front of the cottage. He doesn't see me crying, hands hanging at my sides, lifeless. I'm there watching my husband pull into the street, and turn south, to go to a townhouse off the Five, in a canyon, with a girl waiting there for him inside.

10

GONE

I stand there, in the driveway, not knowing what to do. I don't know how long I'm there. Then the tears come. Hard.

Soon, I'm face down in the driveway, and it's a long time before I care who might see or hear me.

I don't know what to do. By now he is at home in the townhouse. She has greeted him. Hugged him. Her daughter has, too. And I am here, at a beach cottage I made into our home, and I don't know what to do.

He is gone.

I couldn't save him.

I couldn't help him.

I couldn't give him what he needed.

I ruined myself in trying.

I call my mother-in-law. I know as soon as she

answers that I should have waited until I calmed down, but I don't know what to do. I tell her so.

"Are you alone?" she asks.

"Bugsy is here. The dog is here."

"Can you get to your aunt and uncle's?"

I look at the red Fiat and can't imagine driving right now.

"They aren't far," I say.

"Get to your aunt and uncle's, and call me when you get there. You shouldn't be alone."

"Okay," I say. "Okay."

"Take a deep breath, honey. Slow down a little. You're going to be okay."

"I know. I'm so sorry. I'm so sorry."

"Don't be sorry, be strong. You're going to be okay."

"Okay."

"Get into your little car, drive down to your aunt and uncle's, and call me when you get there, okay?"

"Okay. Okay."

I can barely see as I stumble into the empty front room of the cottage. I can barely see as I grab keys, and pajamas, and give Bugsy his dinner.

Be strong, I say to myself, be strong. You are a strong woman. You will be okay. I say all these things to myself.

What I say out loud, to the cottage, to Bugsy, to the trees is, "He's gone, he's gone, he's gone."

I cry on the rug in the main room of the cottage and tell the sand pressing against my forehead that he's gone.

I look in the bedroom and picture us waking up there this morning, husband and wife. I tell the bed he is gone.

I tell the gate on my way out, I tell it as it opens and as it slams shut that he is gone. He is gone.

The Fiat doesn't start, which is good. It stops my crying. I am frantic, I can't stay here. I can't stay here with him gone. I try again, and my little red car comes to life.

I miss the exit to my aunt and uncle's because I am looking for Ben's Jeep. Downtown San Diego is looming in front of me, and I don't know how to get back to where I need to be. We've lived here since September, but I don't know where I need to be. I call my aunt and uncle to tell them I am lost. I call my mother-in-law to tell her I'm almost there. She tells me I'll be okay, and I tell her I love her. I tell her to tell Ben I love him if she talks to him.

I don't sleep. I don't sleep because now I know where Ben is, and who he is with. He isn't at Frankie's. He is with her. I know there is nothing I can do, nothing I can say, nothing I can fix. He is gone. He is with her. I sit on the back deck all night, waiting for the sun to rise. The dew gathers on the deck and on me. It builds until there is a layer on both of us. I am waiting for the sun to rise. Even though I don't know what I'll do when it does, I wait. I wait for the sun, I wait for the day, I wait to know what to do. I call my sister in Chicago and leave a message. I don't know what I have said when I hang up.

I couldn't help him.

I couldn't save him.

I couldn't give him what he needed.

I ruined myself in trying.

He is gone.

11

PHONE RECORDS

Mandy thinks it's a bad idea, my friend Lacey thinks it's a good one. Ben is gone, but I have all of his phone records. All of the phone calls between him and the girl. Five or six a day for two months.

When Ben first told me about the girl he told me not to tell anyone about them because they could lose their jobs if I do. He told me not to tell Beth, their manager. I don't know why he has told me this, because I don't know Beth. I have never met her. But he tells me many times that she can't know about him and the girl.

I have the phone records, and I have the cashier's checks, and I have Beth's name. I am at the Chula Vista office of Ben's company, asking for a woman with the name Beth, with phone records and cashier's check stubs with his name and the girl's name. Ben has told me not to do this, but Ben is gone.

This morning, sitting on my aunt and uncle's deck, I called Ben and left a message. Early. I tell him the reason why he would stay, his reason, not mine, is because he never gave us a chance. For years, because he was hateful, resentful, and angry, he never even gave us a chance.

"So you would stay to be with the girl you fell in love with enough you thought it would last a lifetime. Without the hate. Without the resentment. Without the anger. Just you, and just me."

This is the last time Ben will ever hear my voice. I won't even know if he listens to the message.

I hope he isn't here at the Chula Vista office today but is up north and inland at his office. Even though I'm here, I don't want him to know I've come.

I'm relieved when I see Beth. She seems like me. Or at least how I used to be. Strong. Capable. Sweet.

"I'm Ben's wife," I say.

"I know Ben." She is watching me.

I am about to cry.

"I tell you what, you stay right here, and I'll get tissue and water, okay?"

I nod, in thanks.

I'm embarrassed I have come. I don't know why I have come other than Ben told me not to, and my friend Lacey says she would do it if she were me. Somehow, this was enough.

Beth puts water in front of me, and I drink it. I grab one of the tissues because I know I will need one soon.

"Are you okay?"

I shake my head, no.

"Take your time, just take your time." Her eyes are concerned. This poor girl I've never met. She is worried.

"My husband is having a relationship with one of your employees."

When I say the girl's name, Beth is surprised.

"Are you sure?"

"I brought phone records and the deposit receipt for their apartment."

"I am so sorry."

"I don't know why I'm here, I just want someone to know the truth. I'm sorry."

"Don't apologize, don't even think twice, I don't think anything differently of you for being here." She pauses. "Are you sure they aren't just friends?"

"Well, he told me they have slept together."

"Well."

"I went to Annapolis for my youngest brother's graduation, and he moved out, and they started sleeping together. I was in Annapolis," I say. I don't know why.

"I grew up there!" she says. I think she's glad for the familiarity in this strange conversation. "I'm getting married there later this year."

"That's wonderful. Congratulations."

"Yeah," she looks at me, she's thinking. "You know this is hard for me because my fiancé used to date this girl."

"What is she like?"

"I don't know her that well, really," Beth says. "She just works for me. But my fiancé is a good, good man. I can't imagine him dating anyone who wasn't, too."

"Ben said she had a little girl, three or four years old?"

"She's more like eleven or twelve. She's big."

"Wow."

Ben is a father figure to her little girl, who isn't little. Who will remember Ben her whole life. Ben is part of her life, too.

"I've thought about calling her," I say, "just so she really knows what's going on."

"She knows," Beth says. "I guarantee she knows. Spare yourself the pain."

"I'm so embarrassed."

"Don't be. This isn't how these things work, you know. When someone wants to end a marriage, they sit down and talk about it. You deserve better."

"I know."

"I once found out a man I had been seeing was married." Beth is talking softly. "As soon as I found out he was married, it was over. No questions. I told him if I ever saw his phone number on my caller ID again, that it had better be a woman's voice on the other end."

"Wow."

"As soon as I knew he was married," she says again.

I look at my wedding ring. I hold tight to it while we talk.

We sit for a long time, and it's so nice to be with someone my age. I haven't had girlfriends here in San Diego. Ben never wanted to go out. I've been all on my own since he decided to stop coming home.

"I guess this isn't the first you've heard of this, though," I say when I apologize again.

"What do you mean?"

"I actually did call her once before and told her my marriage was important to me. She said she had been directed not to talk to me."

"By me? She said she was directed not to talk to you by me?"

"I don't know. She just said she had been directed not to talk to me. And Ben said she had come and talked to you about getting a message from Ben's wife, not knowing what to do."

"No."

"It never happened?"

"No."

"Ben said he had been placed on probation, was ordered not to talk to anyone in the Chula Vista office, was taken off his special projects, and ordered to talk to human resources."

She is looking at me, and I know this isn't true, too.

"He's a bad, bad man. You're a lucky girl."

"I can't believe none of that is true."

"I wouldn't even have the power to do any of those things. I can't direct anyone not to talk to anyone else. It just wouldn't happen, and I wouldn't do something like that, either."

"Why would she say she couldn't talk to me?"

"I don't know."

"I'm so embarrassed."

"You know, I can't say I would do the same thing, because I can't imagine what I would do, but I don't think anything less of you for being here," she says again. "Are you going to be okay?"

I nod.

"Take my cell number. Call if you just need someone to talk to. I'll let you know if human resources can do or wants to do anything with these. Are they for me to keep?" she asks of the phone records. I nod.

"Thank you so much," I say and hope she knows I mean it.

"You'll be okay, you'll be so much better off."

"Thank you."

She hugs me and tells me to eat a sandwich. I laugh because I hear this a lot lately, and I promise I'll go get a hamburger. I'm careful going to the elevator and to the car. I don't know what she looks like, but I don't want to see her. I have driven our car, the blue Volkswagen, and I get in and feel free.

I have done something unforgivable. Something Ben has specifically said not to do. Even if he tried coming back again, there would be this. He wouldn't forgive this. I call Mandy and Lacey and tell them what I have done. They are relieved it went well, because it could've gone very, very badly. I agree.

I call Russ, our friend from Kansas who has known Ben since he was a little boy. I tell him what I have done.

"Wow, so what's the latest, other than this?"

"He's living with her. I called his landlord. He's with her and her little girl."

There is silence. I'm not sure if Russ is there.

"Turns out her little girl is eleven or twelve, not three."

There is silence. I wonder if I should ask Russ if he is still there.

"I don't even know who this guy is," he finally says. "I don't think I'll ever talk to him again. I just don't."

"He hasn't answered your calls?"

"No."

"I don't know what to do, Russ."

He is quiet. For a long time, he is very quiet.

"I don't know what to tell ya."

"I don't really want Ben to get fired. That's not why I went. I just wanted someone who knows them both to know the truth."

"You don't have to worry about Ben getting his," Russ says. "God is a just God."

I know he is right. But God also took Ben away from me. God also watched the last two months as I struggled.

My sister has called while Russ and I talk and her message says that she is leaving Chicago after work tomorrow and will be here by ten. When I hear she is coming, I cry. I have been to see Beth, and my sister is coming. It is over, and Ben is gone.

In the early, early morning, I drive our blue car along the Five, turning into every canyon I find, looking for the black Jeep. I need to see it parked in front of the townhouse. I need to see the reality of Ben's life, and that I'm not a part of it. I drive for hours, and am lost over and over again.

On a street named Balboa, just off the Five, in a canyon, there is a complex of townhouses lined in a row. It is almost morning now, and I know I need to give up this ridiculous search. I decide I will picture

Ben here, at this place, even though I can't find his Jeep. I am in a canyon, just off the Five, in the parking lot, facing rows and rows of townhouses. If I get out of the car and yell his name, he might come running out from one of the doors. But I have gone to see Beth, and my sister is coming. It is over. Ben is gone.

12

LEAVING CALIFORNIA

The red Fiat is parked under a light at the San Diego airport, and as my sister and I get closer, it is gleaming in the dark night.

"This is yours?"

"Yep," I smile.

"This is the perfect California car."

"Pretty cool, right?"

"I love it!"

"Do you mind if we have the top down?"

"No! Are you kidding? This is Southern California in July, top down!"

I'm thankful for her enthusiasm at the little red convertible.

The tears had started as soon as I saw her walking down the hallway from the passenger area, and we had held each other crying for a long time before we got to this point. The tears are dry now, and we're two young blondes jumping into the perfect Southern California car. We get noticed before we're even out of the parking lot.

I take my sister up the Five to the cottage, and I'm watching, waiting for the black Jeep. I have had a dream where I saw Ben in his Jeep, with a girl beside him who had long curly hair. I had jumped out of my car in the dream and run after them. They had gone into a movie theater, and in the darkness, I was looking and looking for the girl with long curly hair. When I finally found her, she sat and looked at me, and as she did, hair grew on her face and chest, body expanding to a full, heavy figure.

I don't think she has curly hair, but now I am looking for Ben in the black Jeep I bought him with a curly haired passenger at his side.

"You just leave it open like this?" my sister asks when we get to the cottage.

"It's La Jolla Shores," I say with a shrug. "Not Rogers Park, Chicago."

"Whatever. It's still wide open, and your computer is just sitting out."

"Doesn't bother me."

"It should."

Lying in bed that night, I leave the curtains open,

and the light of the moon is shining in on my sister.
She is fast asleep. I think of Ben and who he is sleeping
beside, and I cry as quietly as I can until I am asleep, too.

We spend the next two days, my sister and I, trying to
figure out what it is I am going to do. We come up with
lists. Get up. Brush teeth. Walk Bugsy. Take Shower.
Look for jobs. Eat. Visit Ma and Papa. Visit Aunt Denise
and Uncle Lon. Visit brother. Eat. Walk Bugsy. Brush
teeth. Go to bed.

We plan out the next month day by day, so I can get
up and know that the first thing I am going to do each
morning is brush my teeth.

We walk to the bench where Ben told me he
thought he loved me and I ask my sister to sit there
for a moment so I can remember her there, smiling. I
am trying to erase the memory of Ben sitting there in
the same spot and replace it with her. Replace it with
someone who will love me and be with me until death
do us part.

"We should go to his family day," my sister says,
hanging up the phone with my brother.

"I really don't want to."

"It would mean a lot."

"A family day where we're stuck on a Navy ship for

hours, no escape, no place to hide. I don't think this is a good idea for me."

"We're going."

"What about the list."

"You can start that when I leave, which is soon, so you're going to enjoy this while you can and be there for your brother."

"The list says I should be looking for a job."

She looks at me. I know we are going.

"You know," she is thoughtful, "this is the first time I've felt like the older sister."

I understand what she means, because even though I'm younger, I have always taken care of her. I have always taken care of her, and of Ben, and of everyone I love. I am the strong one.

We bring sweaters to family day because we don't know what it's like to be on a Navy ship off the coast of California. Maybe it will be cold even though it's July. Our brother is there, in uniform. He looks younger than twenty-five to me. Like he's not old enough to be trusted to steer this ship, even though he is.

We were on this ship for Christmas, eating in the officers' wardroom. Ben was there. He had loved it. I can't stop thinking about how Ben would love this as we pull away from the docks and move into the endless blue of the ocean. We go under the Coronado Bridge, and I think of Ben and how much he would have loved this. We pass Ocean Beach, and I think of Ben and how much he would have loved this. Then I remember he goes to the beach on Fridays now. With her. I watch Ocean Beach for a speck of a person who might be like Ben, but we're too far away.

We make it all the way off the coast of La Jolla Shores, and a whale decides to join us for a while as we turn around to head back to dock.

Ben would have loved this.

I find a women's bathroom through the dark, twisting metal hallways in the humming underside of this great ship, and cry. This bathroom is only big enough to turn around once, with a mirror splashed dirty from the sink. Large metal pipes run through the ceiling, like they do throughout the rest of the ship. The space closes in on me, and I cry.

"Are you doing okay?" our friend Donna asks when I get back above deck.

She has come along for family day and knows about the girl and about Ben.

"Might be feeling a little motion sickness," I lie.

She knows I am lying and smiles.

"You'll be okay."

"I know."

When she hugs me, I say over her shoulder toward

the dancing blue ocean all around, "He would have loved this."

"We're here, though. We love you. We want you here with us."

I know she is right, but it was always my job to show Ben new things. New things like cruising the Pacific on a United States Navy ship.

It's a relief to walk the plank to dry land. I can't get to the car soon enough. There is nowhere for me to go, but I can't stay near this ship any longer.

"We're going to the rodeo," my sister says.

"Today?"

"For a couple of hours. Will you be okay?"

"I don't want to go."

"We'll go just for a bit. They already have tickets."

Ben went to the rodeo last year, while I was in Kansas City. He had loved it.

We go, and in our front box seats with all of my aunt and uncle's friends, I cry. My brother holds me as ambitious California cowboys ride the bulls and are thrown into the air after mere seconds. I know I could hold on longer than that.

"Your niece is crying," I hear someone behind us whisper.

"Her husband just left her," someone whispers back.

I've had enough. I have cried my way through the day on a Navy ship, now here at a rodeo, and I want to go home and cry in peace. I get up to go as my sister says proper goodbyes.

"Are you okay?" one of my aunt's friends asks when I get to the top of the box.

"My husband just left me."

"Hmm. Been there. Him, too," she says, waving a thumb toward the man standing next to her.

"Really?"

"Oh yeah. It probably seems pretty dark right now, but I promise you it gets better."

"Really?"

"It has to."

"It has to," I repeat.

"It worked out for you then?"

"We ended up together, so that's not so bad, right?" She is joking, and I can tell with her smile that she knows my pain.

"You'll be better than you were before this," she says as she hugs me.

"Thank you."

I don't believe her.

My sister is ready to go, and we walk through the stands of people cheering, and yelling, watching another cowboy try his best on top of a bucking, writhing bull.

Ben would have loved this.

"What does your list say?" my sister jokes as we leave.

"Ha, ha."

"Do you think you can handle a beach fire in Ocean Beach?"

"Tonight?"

"When the rodeo is done."

"Are you serious? Isn't this enough for one day?"

"We're getting you back into life," she says.

"Right."

"The world has been moving without you, Jamie, you're not missing anymore."

"Right."

The fire at my brother's is intolerable. There are girls there who are in the kind of pain I am in. Everyone wants to tell their stories.

"We were engaged. I had my daughter start calling him dad, for Christ's sake, and I found on my computer he'd been on this website where you look up girls in your ZIP code and talk to them. A sex website, talk to them, watch video of them."

"Disgusting," someone says.

"It just crosses the line, you know? These are actual people he's up talking to, people he could very well meet or run into."

"I just found out my boyfriend spent the summer in England with another girl," another one says.

She doesn't get as much sympathy as the girl who was letting her daughter call her boyfriend dad.

"This is the third time he's cheated on me," she says.

"I am sick and tired of good girls wasting their time on losers!" My brother has had enough of the fireside chatter.

"Her husband just left her, moved in with another woman, signed a year lease with her, and the woman he's living with has a daughter that's, like, eleven," someone says, pointing to me.

There is silence.

"You win," a girl on my left says.

"Yeah, probably do," I say.

"I was letting my daughter call him dad, though, and he was online in a sex chat room with people in our neighborhood," this other girl says, incredulous.

"Yeah, but they were married," a girl I don't know says from across the fire. "That's different."

I have had enough, and my sister has to fly early in the morning back to her life in Chicago. We get up to go, and my brother's neighbor who knew Ben and me together takes my hand and pulls me down, so I am even with her face. The breeze is blowing the smoke from the fire all around us. We inhale it, she and I, the smoke-filled air between us.

"It's not like he's gone and found this great woman," she says. She is looking me straight in the eye. "He's found someone who is every bit as screwed up as he is. She's nowhere near the woman you are."

I'm thankful for this, and she lets me cry on her shoulder before I stand again to go.

The ship, the rodeo, the fire in Ocean Beach. Ben would have loved them all. But Ben wasn't there. And even if he were, Ben hated going out, so I might have missed them all anyway. I try to be thankful Ben wasn't here so that I could do all of these things, but I miss him. He would have loved this day.

Tomorrow, my sister leaves. I will be left with the lists we made, and Bugsy, in a beach cottage I made into a home for Ben. I will sleep by myself two miles from where Ben is, and I know I can't find him if I try.

Driving back to the cottage after I drop my sister at the airport, I try to enjoy the beautiful day. The sun is shining, and as I come over the hill into La Jolla Shores, the ocean is in the distance dancing and swaying beyond the hilltops. It has been five days since Ben drove away from me, since I last heard his voice. I am alone.

My dad is calling as I walk into the main room of the cottage, and I step around Bugsy sprawled on the rug to get to the desk where my phone is flashing red. For the first time in a week, I will answer and not worry about what to say. Ben is gone.

"He changed the password on our bank account this morning," I tell my dad. "Now I don't have access to pay our bills."

"Change it back."

"I can't," I say. I can't believe Ben has done this, and neither can my dad.

We decide to talk about more pleasant things, and I am telling my dad about the cruise on a Navy ship, and the rodeo, and the fire in Ocean Beach when my phone beeps with another call. I look to see Ben's face framed by the Sonic menu. Husband, my phone reads. Call waiting.

"Dad, it's him, do I get?"

"Hell no, I'm sorry."

My dad doesn't swear often.

"No?"

"You're on the phone with me, we'll finish our conversation, that sonofabitch can wait. I'm sorry."

My dad doesn't swear often.

I am nervous, and when I see Ben has left a message, I beg my dad to hang up so I can hear it.

"Do not call him," he says.

"I won't."

"You call me right back after you hear that message."

"Okay."

I am shaking as I press the buttons to get the message. I have no idea why Ben would call. I think maybe he is calling to talk about the details of a divorce, or separating our lives. Maybe he is calling to tell me he is sorry.

"Hey, it's me." His voice is singsong on the recording. "Bet you noticed I left my pillow there and I was hoping I could drop by and pick it up. Or we could meet somewhere, if you'd rather do that. Also, I'd like the keys to get into storage, I need a few things here so I can unpack. I've been living out of boxes way too long. That's it, talk to you soon. Later."

"Dad." I have called him back right away. "He wants his pillow."

"Tough shit. I'm sorry."

My dad doesn't swear often.

"I think I need to get out of here," I say, looking around the open cottage. The doors and the windows are wide open. I'm not safe here anymore.

"You're going to pack up your things, and get the hell out of there." My father's voice is commanding.

He is still talking, but I'm not listening. I am taking

whatever I can find with my free hand and piling it into bags. Piling into boxes, pushing clothes into suitcases. Books, sweaters, papers, pens, shampoo. It is all getting piled. It is all leaving this place with me.

"I'm packing right now, Dad, I'll call you when I'm done."

"Do that. Your mom or I will be here to answer."

"Dad."

"Yes, Jamie."

"It might be time for you or Mom to come."

They have been waiting for a month, bags packed, ready to help me. I haven't wanted the help. I could handle it all on my own. I could figure out this marriage and my husband on my own. I am twenty-eight years old and a wife, I can figure my life out on my own.

"Your mother will be there tomorrow."

"Thank you, Dad. I love you."

"And we love you. You're going to be okay, Jamie."

"I know."

"Do not call him back."

"I won't."

"Do not, under any circumstances, call him back."

"I won't."

"Call when you're out."

Everything, absolutely everything that is mine fits into the blue Volkswagen that has been hidden around the corner. I have taken everything. Bugsy watches as I balance my last box through the gate, and I know I'll have to come back to care for him. I will come, though, when I know Ben is at work and not stopping by to pick up his pillow.

Ben's pillow is packed in the back of the Volkswagen. He hasn't needed this pillow in two months. He won't need it again.

"Donna?" I'm on the phone, and I can't see out the back of the Volkswagen.

"Can I park my car at your apartment tonight?"

"Sure, whatever you need. Everything okay?"

"I'm moving out of the cottage."

"Okay. Anything I can do?"

"Just need to park my car where Ben can't find it."

"I can do that, no problem."

I call my brother. I will stay with him tonight. We will move the red Fiat to Ocean Beach after we park the blue Volkswagen full of all my things in front of Donna's apartment downtown, where Ben won't find it.

"Mom is coming tomorrow."

"I know," he says. "You're doing the right thing. Finally."

"I know."

Ben calls three more times before my mom gets into town the next morning. One of his phone calls comes while I'm visiting Carolyn, a counselor I started seeing two months earlier.

"It's him," I say, holding up the phone. "I haven't been answering."

"I think that's good," she says.

"Do you mind if I listen to the message?"

"No, please. I'm kind of curious what his voice sounds like."

I hold up the phone between us for her to hear.

"Just me, calling to see if you're still avoiding me. Okie dokie. Bye."

"That's his fourth phone call in twenty-four hours. I didn't get a single call all last week."

"And you haven't been answering."

"No."

"Good. He's taken you on quite the roller coaster ride the last few months."

"I think I need to get off that ride."

"I think you already have. You're ready."

"Why do you say that?"

"Your mom is coming," she says, and smiles gently. "You're finally to the place where you won't put up with what he is doing anymore. You aren't answering your phone when he calls. You know it is done. And not because he says it is, because he's still calling. You know it is done because you are done."

And I am. I am done. Ben is gone. My mom is coming to take me home.

"My dad is convinced Ben is mentally ill." I laugh as I say this. I look down.

"He is."

"Yeah, he is." I laugh again.

"No, Jamie." Carolyn waits for me to make eye contact. "*He is*."

Then the quiet stays for a while.

There is a lot to get into place before Thursday. Our flight to Minneapolis leaves Thursday, softball day. This seems too soon to put everything in order. This seems like it may be impossible. But my mom is ready.

As soon as I see her, I know. She is ready. We sit at a restaurant and make a plan.

"Is this what you want to do?" she asks.

"I don't know what to do. I know I don't want to stay."

"The reality here is that your husband has left you penniless, without a home. You don't have a lot of options. We, of course, want you home. But I need to know that this is what you want."

"I don't know what to do," is all I can say.

"Then I'm taking you home."

I don't know if this is what I want. But I don't know where to go, or what to do, or where or who to be.

"You missed my nose ring," I say, smiling.

"You had a nose ring?" My mother is disgusted.

I smile. "It was cute."

"Thank God your father didn't see it," she says.

We have a lot of work ahead of us, and as we stand from the table to go my mother tells me I'll be okay.

"I know," I say. "I know."

The first thing is a meeting with a lawyer. Back when Ben first disappeared we had found her, a friend of a friend, so that I would be ready if Ben decided he didn't want to be married.

"I'm sorry to see you again," she says. "I guess this means things didn't work out."

I shake my head no.

"The coworker?"

I nod my head yes.

"I'm really sorry. Are you ready to move forward?"

Ben has told me he will never file for divorce, that he is going to let me do it so that I will look like the one who is walking away. So that I will be the one who looks bad. Even though I know it's the aggrieved party who brings legal action in every rulebook other than Ben's, I don't want to be the one here doing this. But I know I can't be married to a man who is living with another woman.

"Yes," I say. "We can move forward."

"Okay. There's paperwork to do, but not too much."

"Can we have this done by Thursday?" my mom asks. "We have a noon flight back to Minneapolis."

"Not a problem."

"That wasn't so bad," my mom says as we step out of the building into the summer sun.

"No," I agree. It wasn't.

I am given three small assignments by my mother before she drops me at my brother's house in Ocean Beach. Buy cat litter for Captain Jack to give to Ma and Papa. Captain Jack is staying in La Jolla. Buy a hard-topped dog crate for Huey to fly in. Huey is coming with us. Find a mover.

The day passes and I don't leave my brother's couch. His phone rings, and I know it is my mom.

"She hasn't moved," I can hear my brother say as he steps outside to the backyard.

They are talking about me. What they will do to take care of me. This poor girl who has lost her husband.

This poor girl who has lost herself.

"I don't know, Mom," my brother says into his phone, looking in at me. "I don't know."

I turn over on his couch and cry. I couldn't move if I had to. I can't think. I'm barely hanging on.

"Did you find a moving truck?" My brother is back in the house. I know he knows I haven't, so I don't say anything.

"Come on, Jame, let's get up and go get some cat litter and a dog crate. It's not that far."

I won't move unless he makes me.

I won't talk unless he makes me.

I won't get up from this couch unless he makes me.

And I don't move.

I don't talk.

I don't get up from the couch.

"Jamie." It's my mom. She has come. "Let's get going."

I don't want to move.

"Have you found a mover?"

I don't want to speak.

I know she knows the answer.

"It's too late for today, but we've got to do better tomorrow. We are out of here at noon in three days. We've got a lot to do."

I don't sleep again, and early, carly, early in the morning, I get up and walk around my brother's backyard. The night is clear, and I can hear the waves crashing a block away. It is only me and the skunks and the stray cats. If there were a tsunami, I think, we'd all be wiped out. That might be nice, I think.

I go out to the front of his house and stand in the street so I can see the glimmer of the waves. Looking up to the dark sky, I talk to God.

"Show me a shooting star if Ben is going to marry her."

Nothing.

"A shooting star if he is thinking of me right now."

Nothing.

"A shooting star if they'll have kids together."

Nothing.

"A shooting star if he is my beloved, my chosen one, and somehow we'll be together."

A bright star tears through the night sky above me, and I laugh. I laugh and I laugh. I laugh and I thank God for his humor. I haven't laughed like this in months. I turn to my brother's house and am asleep before the morning light fills the room.

13

GOING HOME

Before boarding a plane with Huey barking in the underbelly, my mom and I end a life in California. We think of everything, even my name is taken off of the car insurance.

"Can I ask you why?" the girl asks when we go into the insurance office.

"My husband just moved in with his girlfriend and her twelve-year-old daughter," I say.

"That would be a good reason."

"Or a bad one," I smile.

I bring a thank-you note and flowers to Beth at the Chula Vista office of Ben's company. I walk through the main doors, and a girl I have met before as Ben's wife is there in the front lobby with a client. I try to hide my face with the flowers, but it's no use.

"She'll be right back," says the receptionist of Beth.

"Oh, I'll just come back," I say and try to twist my face into an unrecognizable smile.

She doesn't recognize me anyway, and I leave with the flowers and card I have come with.

"What happened?" my mom asks when I get back into the car.

"Someone I once ate a meal across the table from, who should know me, was there with a client."

"Oh no."

"I know."

"What about these flowers?"

"I can't give them to her now. In case she really did know me, then she'd be wondering why I was giving Beth flowers."

"You can still give the card."

"Will you do it?"

I send my mom in to the second floor to turn west off the elevators and ask the receptionist to give the card to Beth, who should be there by now.

"Done," my mom says with a smile when she returns.

"Did you see anyone who might look like they live with Ben?"

"No." My mother laughs. "I didn't see anyone."

We get the dog crate, the cat litter, arrange a time to meet movers in the morning, call storage to be sure they'll be open, call the lawyer to set an appointment.

"What about the car?" my mom asks of the blue Volkswagen.

"I don't want it."

"What are our options?"

"We'll figure it out, let's just keep moving."

And we do. We keep moving until all that is left for us to do the next day is meet the movers at storage, go to the bank to close our shared account, visit the law-yer to sign papers, and figure out what to do with the blue Golf. I'm beginning to think we might actually be on a plane to Minneapolis in two days at noon, and this makes me sad. I still don't know what I want to do. I don't want to leave this life. I don't want to leave, and I don't want to stay.

The movers meet us in the early morning at stor-age, and I drive the blue Volkswagen still stuffed to the brim with all my belongings from the cottage. My mother has come to take me home, and movers are here to take all of my things. All of our things.

We open the two storage units, my mom and I. One with all of the wedding presents, and one with all of our things, and some of the things Ben has claimed as his own.

The movers are speaking Russian to each other. They are my age, and waiting for me to show them which boxes are ready to go. They are talking about me, I think. I know my grandparents told their manager at the moving company why I was moving when he called them to confirm yesterday afternoon. I know they know my husband has left me for another woman. I hope I don't look like someone who would be left like this and try to smile as they talk around me.

The hall is long between the two units, and dark. A window is at the very end, letting sunlight in, but not much. We take everything out of the first unit, and I show the Russians what is mine. Ben's things are piled between the two units on the cool cement floor.

The unit with the wedding presents is easy, in a way. I'm taking them all. Ben has said he wanted to sell them all on eBay, which I know means me selling them on eBay and sending him a check. Of the five guests Ben had at our wedding, only two gave presents, so I decide that the presents are all mine. They all came from my friends and family, anyway.

"He's never touched these plates," my mom says.

"I need plates."

"He hasn't even seen half this stuff," she says.

"I'm taking them."

My mom is glad.

With both units empty, I send everything that is mine down to the moving truck that is waiting in the parking lot where Ben and I just were a week ago, holding each other.

I go through every box of Ben's and find things of mine he has hidden between sweaters and books. A painting that was a wedding present. Files with our tax information. I take them all. I decide from Ben's pile what I want, and put the rest in the empty storage unit that used to hold our wedding presents.

I have taken everything.

"Kind of sad, if this is all you had in life," my mom says, looking at the things we have left for Ben.

He has a bookshelf, a dresser, a bedside table. Boxes of clothes. This is it. I leave a few posters for him that I don't want. When he moved out the third time he had taken all of our wall art.

"I have a lot of wall space to fill," he said of his new apartment.

"Won't you look at this poster of St. Louis and think of me and how I brought you there for your birthday and bought you this poster?" I had asked.

"No. I'll think, I went to St. Louis once."

I leave him the poster of St. Louis in this pile of things.

The blue Volkswagen is emptied, all of its contents piled into the moving truck. And we're done. We drive away from storage, my mom and I, as the movers rearrange and mark all of my boxes in the dark insides of a moving truck they promise we will see again in Minnesota.

We go to the bank. I have been advised by my lawyer to close the account. It's all my money in it right now, anyway, but it seems so mean to me to do something like this.

"Take it from me, and my experience, you want this account closed. Separate yourself financially in every way," my lawyer said.

My mother-in-law has also told me to close the account. My mother has, too. They both know Ben drained the account a month ago, leaving me with nothing.

"I think it's the right thing," the banker says to me, as I study the bank records. She is being very patient as I sit across from her.

"Okay," I finally say, "let's do it."

She clicks away at her computer, as I watch cars go by out the window. We're just off the Five, near a canyon. Maybe Ben is near as I close our account.

"He can change the password on you but now it doesn't matter." My mom is smiling.

I smile back. This just feels mean.

"It's all your money, Jamie."

"I know, it's just strange."

"You're doing the right thing," the banker says, again.

As she clicks away, closing the account, my mom and I make plans for how to get my bike to Minnesota. We have forgotten it, and it's the last thing I have here in San Diego that won't be on an airplane tomorrow at noon.

My mom knows of a bike shop that will dismantle it and prepare it for shipping, and an hour later we are in front of the shop, in a parking lot across from the bank where Ben and the girl got their cashier's checks.

After the bike is dropped off we go to the cottage to walk Bugsy, and my mom is nervous. Ben might come. Ben might come while we're here. He might come, looking for his pillow. He has been calling this whole week. Twelve or thirteen times a day. He doesn't usually leave messages, but when he does, I can hear the increasing exasperation in his voice.

"I guess you don't want to talk to me, and I guess I don't blame you, but I really would like to get into storage so I can unpack. I've been living out of boxes for a long time and it'd be really nice if I could unpack. And you're doing all this stuff I don't know about. You can call me, or you can email, just tell me what's going on."

He doesn't mention his pillow again.

My papa has agreed to walk Bugsy for me twice a day until his owner, Kaus, comes back from India. I write Kaus to tell him I have to go home, and he understands. He knew before he left that things with my husband were precarious.

The sun is setting on us, and my mom is anxious to leave, but I know this is the last I'll see of the cottage. The last I'll see of Ben and me. I stand in the empty main room of the cottage and say goodbye. To the cottage, to Bugsy, to my husband who stood in these rooms and told me he loved me. Then left me crying on the floor.

We have decided to leave the Volkswagen Golf in California. We have decided to leave it at Ben's work, in the parking lot. My mom is in my rearview mirror as we drive inland and north to his office. We pull into the parking lot, and our black Jeep is there. This makes my mom nervous, but I know at this hour, though, it just means Ben has driven a company car home. He does this a lot to save the gas and mileage on his own vehicle. I know we are safe. My mother does not.

I pull the blue Golf in beside the black Jeep, and read again the note I have written Ben telling him of the things I have done, and that should we ever meet again that he would be greeted with the warm embrace of an old friend. I write this knowing I will never see him again, so it's safe to say this little lie. I tell him it was an honor to be his wife. I know we will never speak again, so it is safe to say this kind of lie, too. I am sitting and reading the letter, in my little blue car I have driven all over the country beside Ben in, when my mother knocks on the window.

"Let's get out of here," her eyes are frightened. We don't know what Ben would do if he were here.

"It's okay, Mom," I say through the closed window.

"It is not okay, let's get out of here."

I carefully place the note on the passenger side, with a picture from our wedding, and the storage keys so he can go get his things to unpack.

I leave the key to the little blue car in the glove compartment of the black Jeep, and I look inside and picture Ben and me sitting here.

"Let's go," my mother says from her car.

I am angry. I am saying goodbye. These two cars sat here like this beside each other for so long. These two cars are like Ben and me sitting here. I am saying goodbye to a piece of my life.

My mother is nervous, and when I get in the car I am angry with her.

"Then get out, go sit in the Jeep, if that's what you want to do. Go do it, be quick." Her fear is palpable.

"I'll be fast," I promise and go to the Jeep with Kansas plates, open the passenger door, and sit. I don't sit long, just long enough to think she has probably sat here, too. And the goodbye is ruined with this thought. He can have the fucking Jeep, I think. He can have the fucking Golf, I think. He can have them. I notice the brown splashes all along the blue car as I get out and am glad I didn't wash it.

We drive away, and I watch our two cars parked side by side until we get to the street and leave them there under the lights of an empty parking lot.

We have done it all. Everything is taken care of.

My mother checks her rearview all the way back south, all the way to the coast where we are sleeping tonight. I know Ben isn't following us. Ben is nowhere near. We couldn't find Ben, and he couldn't find us if he tried. He has been calling all night, and a message flashes red on my phone when we get to our hotel. My aunt and uncle have met us and they help my mom with our bags so I can listen to the message. Ben's voice is terse. It is angry.

"Well, it's nice to see that you haven't changed at all. I called my mom and told her of your little tricks, how you are manipulating my family and using them for your own benefit. She knows now, all about your tricks. Nice of you to try and turn my family against me.

It's nice to see you haven't changed at all."

I panic for a moment. He can't take his mother away from me. She's been my strength. She's been my best friend and my confidante. I call her right away. There isn't an answer. I panic. I call again and again. Finally, I leave her a message, and I know she is gone, too.

"She's his mother," my aunt gently says. "This is as it should be."

Early the next morning I call my mother-in-law again. It's not so early where she is. There still is no answer. I am leaving today on an airplane with my dog and my mom. I will sign papers this morning that say "dissolution of marriage." All of my belongings are in a moving truck. I have gone to see Beth. My mother-in-law is gone. Ben is gone. It is over.

We stop for a meeting with the lawyer on the way to the airport. As I sign my married name on a document that reads "dissolution of marriage" at the top, I cry.

"Don't cry, or I'll cry, too!" my mom says, but it's too late. We're both crying.

The office is one large open space and is more like a newsroom than a law firm. It is quiet before one of the lawyers pulls a squirt gun from his desk. "Everyone who cries in this office gets squirted with water." He is joking.

I try to laugh.

I have just signed a paper with my married name that says my marriage is over. In six months, I will get my old name back, and Ben will be free from me forever.

My brother, Ma, and Papa all come to the airport to see us off. Huey is nervous, and my grandparents don't want to see him go, but they'll still have Captain Jack the cat to take care of for me. I am dressed in a black sundress, one I bought last summer and had altered so I would look perfect for Ben. He hated when I wore black, so I always was sure to wear a colorful sweater with it, like I am now. I wore this dress to see Beth. I brought this dress to the cottage thinking maybe Ben and I would go for a nice dinner somewhere. I didn't wear it to dinner with Ben. I have worn it to do something he would never forgive, and I am wearing it now as I leave.

I can't stop the tears, and I don't care, and don't think about all the people who will see. I try to stop them long enough to say goodbye to my brother, Ma, and Papa, who wave on the other side of security as my mom and I weave our way through to the gate. I look back and see them there, waving, but all I really see is Ben standing in the same spot a year before. Standing on the other side of security, waving to me and crying as I leave him to go back to Kansas City. He was crying watching me leave. Where did that man go? Where did my husband go?

We wait to board our plane, and the gate agent calls my mom over to tell her Huey has just boarded and is doing fine. She comes back to me, and I'm crying.

"Why don't you go to the bathroom," she says gently.

"Why?"

"Why don't you just go freshen up," she says.

I cry the whole way. I close the stall door, sink to the toilet and cry. My head is pressed against the cool, hard metal walls of the airport bathroom stall, and I cry.

I don't recognize the face in the mirror looking back at me when I finally unlatch the door and walk into the light of the bathroom. This girl has my clothes on, though. This girl has my wedding ring on. My shoes, my earrings. I don't know who this girl is.

I manage to hold it together down the aisle of the airplane, passing by passengers on either side. The flight is full. I am surprised so many people are willing to leave San Diego to go to Minneapolis. I am still not sure that I am willing. I am numb as we sit and wait to pull away from the airport. I am leaving California. I am not going the way I came. I had to have my family find a way out for me. I had to have my mother pack my bags and take me home.

We lift into the sky, and soon Ocean Beach is below us, then clear blue water, then the green of Balboa Park, where Ben and I came from Kansas City to live on Park Boulevard. I can see the whole city, and with my forehead pressed to the hard plastic window, I look as far as I can. Ben is down there in this disappearing landscape, living his life without me. Ben is down there, somewhere in this green, brown, and blue mangle of land. Ben is part of the buzzing and moving below me. He is there, hidden in broad daylight. My husband is gone. He is gone.

I couldn't find him if I tried.

14

KANSAS CITY

It's late October, and Kansas City is still warm enough to get by without a coat. The warm sun is a relief from the colder Minnesota days. When I land, the airport welcomes me like a living time capsule. Like stepping into my life as it was before. Before California. Before the darkness.

I'm driving through the black night between the airport and the city, and I'm moving slowly. My rental car has Missouri plates and I feel a little bit like an imposter, but I'm glad to pretend like I belong here again.

The hotel I'm staying at is walking distance to our old home, and I know it's a matter of time before I make my way to go sit on our old front steps.

There are things to do before that, though. My friend Lacey is getting married on Saturday, and I'm here for her.

It's early enough after I check into the hotel to go back out into the city. The microbrewery Ben and I loved to sit and play cards at is just a few blocks away. When I get there, I'm tempted to order like we always used to—"one raspberry and one brown beer, please"—but I only order the raspberry for myself.

"Just you?" the bartender asks.

"Yeah," I reply, thinking he should know better than to ask.

The couple on my left is talking quietly. They are very serious as they reach for their beers, eyebrows furrowed as they light each other's cigarettes. Their smoke wafts over me toward a woman to my right who is also alone, and this makes me feel better. I try to be interested in the television above the bar.

Soon, the woman on my right is joined by someone and I want desperately to order the brown just so that there will be two drinks in front of me. "One raspberry, and one brown," I want to say. Just like I used to.

The noise of the bar grinds against my silence, and I finish my raspberry beer in gulps and go to the bathroom. Everything is as I left it. The beer is the same, the bartenders are even the same, the slight smell of mold and cigarettes is the same, the bright yellow lights of the bathroom are the same. For a moment I pretend Ben is waiting for me, and I take time to fix my hair and pinch my cheeks for a little color. But I know he's not there. I don't know where he is. He is gone.

I walk through the bar to the front door with my eyes to the wooden, creaking floor. I'm afraid of what ghosts may be lurking if I look up. I'm afraid of who I might see who will ask where my husband is.

I drive around our old neighborhood before I go back to the hotel. Everything is the same. Everything. Except I'm here now, and Ben isn't, and California is in between. I can't help but cry.

The streets are empty by the time I make it back to the hotel, but I'm not interested in sleep. It has been suggested several times over that Ben likely had an assortment of mental health issues, and I spend the night reading books about bipolar and borderline personality disorders. I have spent the last two months reading about things like this.

"How's the hotel?" my mom asks the next morning. "Did you sleep well?"

"Well enough," I tell her, and it's true.

"How are you?" she asks, and I tell her I'm okay. This is what I will tell everyone this weekend when they ask.

"How are you?" my friend Jenne asks when I pick her up for a morning coffee.

"I'm okay," I tell her, just like I told my mom. "Better than I was." And this is more truthful than anything I could say.

"If you don't want to talk about it," she starts.

"No, really, I don't mind at all. I don't have any lines anymore, there's nothing you can cross," I smile at her. I know she is curious. She's watching me closely as she squints in the sun. We're in the corner of a coffee shop in Kansas, where we used to come and talk about my wedding plans.

"What do you want to know?" I offer. I smile again.

"What happened?" she says wide eyed, shaking her head. "I have to say, I couldn't have been more shocked than if you told me you were giving birth to an elephant."

I laugh at this. Really laugh at this.

She says something Father Mike, the priest who married Ben and me, said when he came to visit me. "I keep going over things in my mind to figure out what it was that I missed."

I'm glad to hear that I wasn't the only one surprised.

"He just stopped coming home," I tell her. "The first night I called the hospital, police, sheriff, the jails, emergency rooms, I had no idea what happened, and he came home around seven in the morning like nothing had happened."

"Shit," she says, shaking her head. "A girl?"

"A coworker."

"I'm so sorry."

"At least it happened quickly. It was literally over-night, so I was spared some pain at least."

"But you stayed for awhile, didn't you?"

"Almost two months. I was waiting."

"For what?"

I smile before I answer, because I know now how ridiculous I sound.

"I was waiting for Ben. Stupid, I know."

"Not stupid," she's kind enough to respond. "He's your husband."

"What do you know about rigor mortis?" I ask.

She's surprised by my question. It's out of left field.

"It happens after you die? Why on God's great earth would you ask?"

"Remember when Zadie died?" I ask, knowing she remembered well when my first cat died.

"Sure."

"Remember when Lola died?" I ask, knowing she remembered well when my puppy died just three months later.

"Sure." she is confused.

"The only explanation Ben gave when Lola died was that she was doing what Zadie was doing, and I've been trying to figure out if maybe that he meant some-thing like rigor mortis."

She is quiet. The coffee shop is quiet. The bell rings on the door announcing a new customer, and Jenne crouches low to the table.

"Do you think he killed them?" she whispers.

I am quiet. Animals were never happy in our home and this is something I've been thinking about for two months. I've been thinking over and over about the last time Huey saw Ben. It had been weeks since Ben had been home but coming back from my grandparents' house on a beautiful late spring evening, Huey knows Ben is inside our apartment before I even open the door. I turn the key and feel the tug on my arm as Huey tries pulling away. He does not want to go inside.

"Sit," I am harsh with him. I see the fear in his eyes. He does not want to be here.

Huey won't come in.

I am angry with myself for bringing him, now that Ben is here.

He is here.

"Hello?" I call out. I am trying to breathe.

Ben is here.

He is here.

There is no response.

I try tugging Huey's leash, to drag him inside. He resists with all his strength, front paws stretched out before him, neck firm in his collar. All thirty pounds of this little patchwork dog are united against me and this apartment.

Huey won't look at me.

It is starting to smell sulfurous and rotten. Like a skunk, Huey's fear seeps into the air. I am familiar with this smell. The smell is here now, growing stronger, and Huey won't come inside.

Ben appears at the door and there is nowhere for Huey to hide. I watch Huey try to back away, twisting in every direction, but there is nowhere for him to go. He can't escape. He sinks to the ground and rolls over. He offers his white belly up to Ben.

"Fucking dog," Ben says, pushing open the door I have half open and stepping around him and away from both of us.

With the clang of the front gate, Huey is snapped back to life. He whines at me as I turn to watch Ben drive past, phone to his ear.

I think about this last meeting but I don't tell Jenne about it now. There is no time. I have been quiet too long, but I still am not ready to answer her question.

"Zadie was doing what Lola was doing," she says to break the silence, "what does that mean?"

"I don't know," I shake my head, "Zadie, Louie, Harlie, Lola, and Huey dead or injured in under seven months."

"Shit."

"I know. I never actually saw him hurt any of them though, so I don't know what to think," I say. My coffee is still hot, so I blow on it and try not to look up at her. "When I first came home and found Zadie and saw she couldn't move, I remember asking Ben what he had done."

"What did he say?"

I focus on grains of sugar that have fallen on the brown table and shake my head. "I remember him looking up from his video game and I was standing there, holding her limp body. She could only move her head a little, and he looks up and says 'What kind of a monster do you think I am?' Then his eyes welled up with tears."

Jenne is quiet.

I let out the breath I am holding. "I think I probably should have left then," I say. And smile. We sip on our coffees and Jenne slides her plate closer to me, offering a piece of her chocolate croissant.

"There was a dog in La Jolla, Bugsy. Bugsy really liked Ben."

"Because Ben was only there for three days."

We laugh. Not the kind of laugh that comes with the idea of giving birth to an elephant, but we still laugh.

"What have you been doing?"

"Well." I sit back and let out a deep breath. The coffee shop still looks the same as before. I look around, the gleaming glass cases with pastries, the chalkboard menu. "I wake up every day and I'm crying before my eyes open."

Jenne doesn't know what to say.

I shrug. It's the truth.

"I try to figure out how rigor mortis affects animals." I smile as I say this. "I read about bipolar and borderline personality disorders, go to the coffee shop every day, see a doctor once a week." I smile again. "Three weeks ago I had my first social outing and met Rachel for lunch."

"Rachel?"

"Handed out programs at our wedding."

"Right."

I didn't talk to Rachel about any of this. Only the rigor mortis part, and she promised to ask a friend who was a veterinarian. Other than that, when she asked how I was, the tears came so quickly I couldn't speak.

"It's okay, it's okay," she had said quickly, "we'll just have a girls' lunch."

I had smiled my thanks.

"Dr. Miller, the doctor I've been seeing, he says what you can mention you can manage," I tell Jenne. "So I guess I've just been trying to say it all. Sorry."

"Don't be sorry."

"I'm still figuring things out. But I'm okay, really."

We talk the rest of the time about her, and as the sun moves across the table and slips onto the floor we know it's time to go.

"Take care of yourself," Jenne says when I drop her off. She is bent down into the car saying this, coffee cup in hand. "Keep me updated."

I promise her I will.

"I'm okay," I tell her with a smile.

She smiles back.

"I'm okay," I tell my friends at the bridal luncheon later. I know better now than to tell them about my investigation into rigor mortis. Lacey is getting married, after all.

"I'm okay," I say again and again. I smile. I tell them I'm okay. "Can you believe she's getting married?" I offer, hoping to change the look in their eyes.

"She's the first since you got married!" someone says, pointing to me. I smile.

"You had a beautiful wedding," my friend Mandy says. "It was so much fun."

"It was beautiful," I say. And it was.

"You two were like Barbie and Ken."

"Thank you," I say.

I smile.

There is silence.

No one knows quite what to do with me. I'm back in Kansas City, with California between us. My husband is gone. He is gone. Their eyes say all of this. They don't know what to do with me.

"Are you okay? Really?" Mandy asks me, champagne glass tipping as she leans in to ask.

"Really," I smile.

It will be another four months before I'll be truthful with this response.

Later, after the toasting, and the gifts, Mandy is happy and full of champagne. I drive her home and listen to her tell about her appendectomy.

"It was worse than going to the girlie doctor!" she shrieks. We laugh.

"I've been twice this summer, that's just how bad my life got." I'm still laughing.

"What?" She's appalled.

"Did I tell you about the adult personals?"

"Um, no. You?"

"No, Ben."

I'm laughing, and even though I know it's from embarrassment, it's a deep, true laugh.

"Stop it."

"We have a shared email account he never changed

the password to, and so I saw he took out an ad on an adult personals website."

"Nice."

"That's my husband," I say with a smile.

"Who is this guy?"

"There's something seriously wrong, I think."

"Um, yeah."

"Yeah." We're quiet for a moment. "So after I saw the ad, I went and got every test in the book."

"Good," Mandy says, loud.

We laugh. We really laugh, and I'm glad.

Sitting in the dimmed basement of the women's clinic at the University of Minnesota waiting for my exams, I laughed, too. Looking down at my clasped hands, I laughed. It was quiet in the waiting room, save a Spanish-speaking woman trying to understand her translator and the nurse explaining she would need to see another doctor.

I had stopped laughing in case maybe they thought I was laughing at them. Glancing over at the nurses at the brightened check-in desk, I was glad to see I was unnoticed. The escalators down the hall were moving in silent unison, one up, one down. I pushed down my skirt and tried not to laugh while I waited for them to call my name.

"You're here for some tests?" the nurse asked once my name was called.

"Yes," I smiled, hoping she didn't know which ones, feeling like I should explain if she did.

The room was quiet, with clean-as-new floors. I wondered if I would have felt better if I had worn my wedding ring.

"I found out my husband has an ad on an adult website," I tell the doctor when she comes in.

She doesn't say anything.

"You know, the kind where they're just looking for sex?"

"I know." She smiles at me. "You'd be surprised how many women I see because of this."

This makes me feel better.

When she finishes, she sends me down the hall and around the corner for an HIV test. I walk quickly.

"Last name?" the new nurse asks.

I think for a moment.

"Johnson?" I ask. "Maybe Patterson?"

She looks at me over her glasses.

"I'm sort of between last names," I tell her.

"Pick one." She has no time for these things.

When I go home and show my parents the Band-Aid on my arm, I laugh again.

It is the same day as Huey's surgery to remove a

mass on his neck that we think grew from years of having Ben yank on his leash. We take pictures, me with my
Band-Aid and Huey with his shaved neck, and we laugh.

Laughing now with Mandy about sitting in quiet
waiting rooms and reading personal ads posted by your
husband is different.

When she gets out of the car, she asks me if I'm
okay. I smile.

"I'm getting there," I tell her. And it's true.

Lacey's wedding is beautiful. She's thought of everything, and my job as personal assistant is an easy one.
In addition to running around placing flowers, holding rings, and making sure the groom doesn't see the
bride before the ceremony, I've been specially assigned
by Lacey's childhood friend to secretly check a camera
recording the whole ceremony from the balcony of the
church.

Once Lacey and her dad slowly make their way up
the stairs to the main floor of the church to turn and
walk slowly through the doors toward her waiting
groom, I run upstairs to the balcony. The red recording light to the camera is on, and I kneel on the floor
behind it watching the room from above.

From this distance it's simply a bride, and simply

a groom. Holding hands and facing each other in front of the altar, promising forever. Promising to love until death.

"This is a marriage. God is supposed to be present, so where's God in all of this?" I had asked Father Mike.

"I can't answer that for you," was all he offered.

Looking down on the pews full of dresses and suits, I wonder if God is here now. Does he see Lacey and her groom down there? Does he hear their promises? Did he hear mine when I made them to Ben? Mostly, I wonder if he heard Ben's promises to me.

I heard Ben's promises on a day much like this. Wearing a dress much like Lacey's. In a room, in front of an altar, in front of a priest much like this.

Father Mike was the priest who married us. When he came to visit, we sat in my parents' backyard in silence not knowing where to start. The day glistened off the pool in front of us, the green of the swaying trees chattering all around.

Finally.

"How are you?"

"Not good."

"I'm here to listen."

And he does.

"I don't know." I shake my head. The water in front

of us is sparkling blue. "It seems like something was very wrong."

"Yes."

"And I meant it when I said for better or worse, I meant my vows."

"I don't doubt the seriousness with which you said your vows. I was there. I know. But there are limits."

I am surprised to hear him say this.

"Limits?"

"There are limits to even the most solemn vows."

The glow from the sanctuary below is bursting with life.

I crawl to the ground and cry. My forehead and nose are pressed into the red carpet, and I move my hands over my mouth. The tears won't stop, and I hear Lacey saying her vows. I can't breathe.

"Till death do us part," I hear her say.

I cry.

"In sickness and in health," I hear him say.

I cry.

"You're okay, you're okay, you're okay," I tell myself.

"You're missing it," I tell myself.

And I do. I miss it. I miss all of it.

"I'm okay," I tell my friends when they see my red eyes. "I can't believe she's married!" This is an acceptable response. I wasn't the only one crying during the ceremony.

Later, much later, after the dinner, champagne, and toasts. After the bride and groom swirl around the dance floor, and kiss, and offer thanks, I drive in the night to our old home near The Country Club Plaza.

It's not very far from the reception, and I pull up in time to see some of the staff from the mid-rise leaving for the night.

"What are you doing here?" Dale asks, arms wide for a hug. Dale was the doorman while Ben and I lived here. Dale watched and smiled as we hauled box after box of wedding presents up to our sixth-floor home.

"Had to come say hi." I smile. "How are you?"

"Fine, fine. Where's that man of yours?"

I smile at him.

I say nothing.

"Oh," Dale says. "Say no more. I don't want to know."

"He left me," I tell him.

"Man."

"But you, you look great! And you're here?" I say, upbeat.

"I am here. I can't believe it's been another year."

"You'll be here when I come back again?"

"At this rate."

"I'll look for you then," I tell him.

I know I won't come back.

When Dale leaves, I sit on the benches just to the right of the front door. I have the patio to myself, and I'm glad for the solitude. From here on the black iron garden chairs, I can see where Ben and I began. The Country Club Plaza is directly across Brush Creek, which runs in front of our building, and I can see the footbridge that crosses to the plaza over splashing fountains that sing into the night and send the creek water into a bubbling frenzy. The ghosts of Ben and me are dancing across the bridge, laughing, spinning, running to the end, where we fall into our first kiss on the stairs.

"What do you want from me?" I ask the night air.

"I'm here now," I say. "What do you want from me?"

Silence.

The ghosts of Ben and me are pulling up into the driveway in our Jeep and our blue Volkswagen, walking by with groceries, dashing past with Huey in tow.

The ghost of Ben is standing in front of me, next to his packed Jeep, ready for his drive to California.

"I don't want to leave you," he's saying.

"Then don't," I tell him.

"I'll come for you in two months," he is saying.

I am seeing the scenery of our beginning.

I am watching the beginnings of our end.

Endings rarely announce themselves.

They steal in and go nameless until long after their work is done.

"What do you want from me?" I ask the night again.

The gravel from the courtyard ground grinds beneath my high heels. My dress is beginning to fail as a source of warmth.

"I'm here," I say again.

"Show me everything is going to be okay," was the first thing I had demanded from the night sky and God. Months before. Before I knew about the girl, but after Annapolis, when Ben moved out the first time.

One block from the Pacific in the heat of early summer, I asked God to show me I would be okay with a shooting star. He answered immediately. I watched, frozen, as a star streaked the dark, early morning sky.

Now, sitting in front of our old home, with The Country Club Plaza and our beginnings sprawled out before me, I'm looking up at the dark early morning sky again.

"I'm here," I say again.

"Tell me Ben still loves me," is the second thing I had demanded of God. I asked this of him in the airport as I left Annapolis. I asked God to have Ben's name paged overhead. When I landed for my connecting flight in Chicago, God answered.

"But I asked and I got a response," I tell my youngest brother when he says it may not have been God saying that Ben still loved me. "It was so specific."

"All I'm saying is that it might not have been God saying Ben still loves you, as much as it was God saying to you that even in the face of this wickedness, I am here. You will find me here."

"Talk to me through the next words I hear." This is the third thing I had asked of God. Sitting at my childhood lake in Minneapolis, face turned to the summer sun, I had made this final audacious demand.

"Don't cry," was the immediate and final response.

I am thinking of all these things, and by now the traffic in front of our home in Kansas City has slowed to a sporadic pop. The sky seems darker with the deepened silence. Ben is easily conjured to sit beside me, feet reaching for a chair to use as a foot stool, hand clutching a glass beer bottle, Huey beneath our feet.

"I'm here now," I tell the Ben I see sitting beside me. "I'm here."

Instead of asking the cooling night air again what it is it wants from me, I think over and over:

Everything will be okay.

Even in the face of this I am here.

Don't cry.

Don't cry.

And I don't.

I don't cry again. Not like I had, and not like I ever will again.

On my way to the airport the next morning, I decide to go back to our home. It's pouring rain and cold, and I'm tired from such little sleep. The parking spot I abandoned just a few hours earlier is still there, and I jump out of the car into the rain to run the short distance to the front door.

It's still too early on a weekend for the building staff to be there, so I'm alone again in front of our home. Under the long blue awning, the rain is falling all around, jumping up from the brick walk to splash against me.

"I'm here at our beginning," I say this quietly. I try not to move my lips. Partly because it's so cold now with the rain, and partly because it's getting just light enough for people to see if they looked down from their homes above me.

"I'm here now," I say for the last time.

The air is damp and full as I breathe it in. The flowers lining the front walk are still bright red despite the fall air, and the chill from the rain. I know they can't possibly be but they look like the flowers I left last summer. The flowers that drifted past as we pulled slowly out of the driveway to meet our future in California.

The red flowers frame the scenery of my memory.

"I'm here," I say to the morning light before me, "I'm here. Do what you will."

15

MINNESOTA

One year later

A year later and it's my last visit with Dr. Miller, the doctor I've been seeing once a week since my parents realized I needed more help than the fresh air up at the cabin and brought me back to my childhood home in Minneapolis. He is just older than my parents with glasses and a full beard. Today he has worn a southwest-style tie with his blazer and is smiling, as always, as he greets me. The timing of this last meeting is perfect because I just got an email from Ben and I'm not sure if I've reacted properly.

Even though I haven't heard from him once since I left San Diego, Ben has now written to say he is sorry. He has written to say there are no words to describe his regret. The move from Kansas, the new job, the stresses of life that followed were too much. He can't explain except to say he was crazy. He is sorry and I have stayed in his heart.

Dr. Miller's narrow office is filled with the light of mid-afternoon in the fall and, as I tell him this news, he smiles and leans back in his chair, nearly hitting the desk on his left and the bookshelf on the right.

"And how did you respond?"

I laugh and feel the undeniable pulse of truth as I reply,

"I didn't. I don't care."

Dr. Miller nods, smiling. I can see his relief.

We've been through a lot together, Dr. Miller and I. I mention that the small, cramped office on the seventh floor of this hospital in downtown Minneapolis has been where I was forced to face hard truths.

"What truths would those be?" Dr. Miller asks.

I want to wait until I have an answer, and he usually allows the silence between us. This time, though, he doesn't wait.

"A few things might be how fine the line is between mental health and unwellness."

"For me as well as for Ben," I interrupt.

"For anyone," he says, arms opening wide as he does.

We smile and I think for a moment I'll be very sad not to come sit on this fading orange couch again.

"And that you've learned how deeply meaningful marriage is to you and how loyal you are. Both good
things that you'll be able to recognize and manage."

I am glad to hear these things named and spoken
out loud.

He leans forward in his chair, an arm swinging a
finger near my face. "To put yourself first and that you
have limitations!" He is enjoying this, now. And so am I.

"You will fail in life!" he declares with a smile,
hand raising a pointed finger to the ceiling. "Accept
these failures. Accept them! And enjoy them as much
as your successes—there is much to learn."

"I know, I know," I smile. "Thank you so much."

"It was a pleasure, Jamie," he says, and I know this
is another truth. I'm the ideal patient because, after all
this time and all the hard work, I am about to become a
former patient.

When the hour ends he walks me out and I think
of the first appointment, sitting with my mother waiting to be called. We waited in the beige waiting room,
which is very much like what I had imagined sitting
in waiting for news on Ben after we rescued him and
placed him in mental health care.

In reality, though, I was the patient in the end.

I was the one who was lost.

I was the one who was brought by my family to be

taken care of when it became clear I needed more than they were equipped to give.

Dr. Miller and I embrace in a quick, awkward hug.

"You take care," he says.

And for the first time in the last hour, tears spring to my eyes. I want to say something meaningful here, like how he helped me to realize what I was searching for. How all along I had thought I was looking for Ben when what I needed to find was myself and the truth inside of me. And to learn how to honor that. The pain in my throat keeps the words from open air.

"Thank you," I manage.

"You're welcome."

And with that, he turns to his next patient, who has just been buzzed through the thick security door. This heavy door reminds me that I'm in the psych unit of a city hospital.

I laugh at this and then smile at the receptionist who is sitting behind a glass window, like you'd find at a bank.

"Take care," I say to her, and walk out. I ride the elevator down seven stories, walk past a security guard on the right, push a heavy glass door open, and step into the cool Minneapolis air.

A breeze picks up, lifting my jacket, whipping my hair across my face, and hundreds, thousands of leaves are flying off trees like avalanches of yellow, green, and brown. They sound like rain as they drop to the sidewalk and I look up at the heights they came from, nearly reaching Dr. Miller's seventh-floor office. The wind is dancing in tree branches, sending them swaying, sending their leaves falling, twirling, spinning, falling. But the trees stand. The trees stand still.